I'M TIRED OF BEING ORDINARY, ARE YOU?

WM. ALLEN

ARE YOU TIRED OF BEING ORDINARY?

If you are tired of being ordinary and want to change your life, or if life is forcing you to transform yourself, this book will help you.

I designed this book to be an entertaining and easy read, but your path from ordinary to extraordinary is not going to be easy. However, if you want it badly enough, you can do it.

Each week, you will work on a trait in your life that will take you from ordinary to extraordinary. The weekly chapters start with a related joke followed by a brief description of the trait you'll be working on. After that is a quote that you can copy and post somewhere to keep yourself focused. Finally, there is a movie suggestion that is not only entertaining, but also illustrates the trait.

Some chapters you will find to be easy while you will have to repeat others a number of times. Do not get discouraged; this is not going to be a quick fix. The weekly chapters cover physical, character, social, and learning traits, as well as some miscellaneous items associated with being extraordinary.

So, how badly do you want to be extraordinary? Do you want it enough to buy this book and try my approach?

ABOUT THE AUTHOR

I am not famous or even well known. I'm just an ordinary guy, who grew tried of being ordinary and thought I could change, as well as help other people who felt like I do to also change

Most of my life, I felt rather ordinary. As a child, I was often one of the last ones picked to be on a team. I was a complete zero in high school and joined the US Army at seventeen. It took me ten years as a part-time student to graduate from college. My climb up the corporate ladder was agonizingly slow, as I continued to read various self-help books practically nonstop.

I did have moments of feeling extraordinary, as I am sure you have had. I ran a half marathon in Scotland. While in the US Army, I served in Iran and Vietnam. I eventually rose to the level of director in a large corporation before retiring in 2009.

Upon retiring, I had time to reflect on my life, my readings, and the exchanges I had with people who commented back to me during the thirty years I sent out "thoughts for the week". Based upon all that, I wrote this book describing traits I believe that, if practiced diligently, can help you become extraordinary.

I'M TIRED OF BEING ORDINARY, ARE YOU?

WM. ALLEN

Harmony Books & Films, LLC

Harmony Books & Films, LLC
602 W. Houstonia Ave.
Royal Oak, MI 48073
248-894-0045

First Edition

Printed in the United States of America by Harmony Books & Films, LLC, Royal
Oak, Michigan

ISBN-13: 978-0990388692
ISBN-10: 0990388697
Library of Congress Control Number: 2014940257
Harmony Books & Films, LLC , Royal Oak, MI

This book is dedicated to Smarty,
a most extraordinary cat.

TABLE OF CONTENTS

ACKNOWLEDGMENTS

I owe a great debt of gratitude to all the people who went out of their way to teach me something about life over the years. I am sorry if I was not always appreciative in those moments.

I owe my thanks to all of you who received any of the weekly thoughts I sent out for thirty consecutive years and encouraged me to continue that effort by either saying you appreciated them or by commenting on what I had sent out.

I also want to thank the following extraordinary people who reviewed and commented on the weekly chapters:

Carol Allen
Carolyn Cruse
Judith Condon
Tania Jann

WARNING—DISCLAIMER

I wrote this book to both entertain you and provide you with ideas on how you can make your life something other than ordinary. This book is not a substitute for advice from qualified professionals such as doctors, lawyers, accountants, physical trainers, etc. Neither is the purpose of this book to provide you with all of the information on any one of the many different traits and topics discussed.

If you want to be extraordinary, you have to accept the consequences of going down this path, and there *will* be consequences. Some of these you may believe beneficial while others may make you wish you had remained an ordinary person. Therefore, the author and the publisher expressly disclaim responsibility for any adverse effects, damages, or losses arising from the use or application of the information contained in this book.

INTRODUCTION

"Whoever said, 'It's not whether you win or lose that counts,' probably lost."

Source: Martina Navratilova
Tennis World Champion

This book describes fifty-two traits that will take you from ordinary to extraordinary. I realize fifty-two may sound like a lot of traits for you to master. However, I suspect that many of these traits are already second nature to you; otherwise, you would not have picked up this book. Therefore, mentioning many of the traits will simply serve as a reminder rather than something you will struggle to master.

Each week you will work on a new trait, or you will make a fresh start on a prior trait that you found challenging. I understand it only takes twenty-one days to make a habit, so please stay with any trait that you are having problems mastering. In time, it will become second nature to you. Do not beat yourself up for encountering a trait that is particularly challenging. It is just part of the process. Stay with it, and you will become more and more extraordinary.

I start each weekly trait with a joke related to the trait. What is the point if you don't have a little fun along the way? Next, I will describe the trait briefly, but only out of respect for your time. You can do further research if you want to know more about a particular trait. Next, I provide a quote that you can copy and post to keep you focused. Finally, I suggest an entertaining movie that will give you something to consider regarding that trait.

What I am asking of you requires change. If you are willing to change, this book will serve as your guide. And remember: it is never too late to change. Don't give up regardless of your age or situation. Ask yourself daily, "How badly do you want it?"

After you become familiar with this book and the traits described, you may wish I had commented upon other aspects of these traits, or you may have come across a quote you feel is more motivational, or you have seen a film that better illustrates a trait. If so, please email me your suggestions at HarmonyBooksFilmsLLC@ comcast.net or visit http://harmonybooksfilms.com/

PHYSICAL TRAITS

Honor Thy Temple

WEEK 1:

Diet—Eat Healthy

A father says to his son, "And what will you do when you grow up to be as big as me?"

Son replies, "Diet."

Ordinary people are killing themselves with the food choices they make, and they are going to pay a heavy price for those choices in their later years. Their joints will not be able to support their enormous bulk. They will end up with knee replacements, diabetes, heart attacks, strokes, and so on. Their quality of life diminish with each meal. The old saying is so true: "You are what you eat."

Restrictive diet plans are not the answer in the long run, and I would be skeptical of any diet plan that promises a weight loss of more than two pounds a week. Oh sure, you may lose considerable weight initially; but as time goes on, it will all return. The best way to lose weight is to make permanent lifestyle changes by saying no to white flour and sugars. Have you ever noticed how much people push desserts on to other people, and often those doing the pushing are overweight themselves?

As important as it is to know what not to eat, it is just as important to know what to eat. There are many conflicting opinions on what you should eat, and new information is constantly surfacing. Also, I think it is entirely likely that when it comes to food, one size does not fit all. Therefore, I will just let you try to stay current on what you should be eating and by experimenting; you will likely find which foods work best for you.

I think the following suggestions may help you stay healthy and energized. First, the less processed food you eat, the better. Second, save restaurants for special occasions and cook most of your meals at home. Third, minimize your salt intake as much as possible. Fourth, drink lots of water. And fifth, never skip breakfast. But make sure it is a healthy breakfast. Some people do well by eating small meals and a few healthy snacks throughout the day so they are never too full or too hungry.

You should eat to be healthy and energized; trying to become thin should not be the goal. Of course, it is possible to eat very little and become thin. But being thin is not the same thing as being healthy and energized. When you lose weight by not eating, you are probably losing muscle as well as fat. Not eating encourages your body to store fat.

Remember—what you eat will always trump exercise. It is very difficult to offset poor food choices with exercise. Exercise provides a great many benefits, but rarely does it result in weight loss without you also modifying your eating habits.

Sadly, some of us are simply predisposed to being overweight. Regardless of our efforts to eat properly and get plenty of exercise, we remain overweight. It isn't fair; it is simply how it is. However, that is no excuse to eat and drink anything we feel like and avoid exercise. You don't have to starve yourself to keep from being seriously overweight. However, it helps to avoid white flour and sugars, manage your portion sizes, drink lots of water, and avoid late-night eating.

Be extraordinary by eating healthy but not to excess.

"To lengthen thy life, lessen thy meals."
Source: Benjamin Franklin

Diet Film: *Eat Drink Man Woman*
Distributed by The Samuel Goldwyn Company

(A senior chef lives with his three grown daughters; the middle one finds her future plans affected by unexpected events and the life changes of the other household members. Description source: IMDB)

WEEK 2:

Exercise—The Components of Fitness: Cardiovascular, Strength, and Flexibility

My grandmother started walking five miles a day when she was sixty.

She is now ninety-seven,

and we don't know where she is!

If you don't have your health, nothing else really matters. However, for most ordinary people, everything matters more to them than doing what they need to do to stay healthy. How many times have you heard someone say, "This dessert is to die for"? Well, there may be more truth in their words than even they suspect. How about those people who say they need to get in shape for the beach or lose some weight for upcoming wedding photos? Extraordinary people stay in shape so that they are always ready for whatever life tosses at them. But many people take better care of their cars than they do their own bodies. Think about the effort people put into making money, only later to find that they would give up every dollar they have to get their health back.

I'm sure you get the point. If you want to be extraordinary, you need to achieve a reasonable level of fitness. There are three components to fitness.

The first component of physical well-being is cardiovascular health. You can accomplish this by movement, such as walking, riding a bike, using a treadmill, or running. You have no doubt heard the term "movers and shakers." Well, if you want to be "a mover and a shaker," it helps if you actually move.

How much do you need to move? Most authorities recommend a minimum of thirty minutes a day. You may be telling yourself that you don't have time to exercise every day, let alone thirty minutes a day. Well, that is what ordinary people say to themselves, but extraordinary people don't find time for what is important; they make time. You can do this by learning to say no to lower-priority activities or delegating those activities because your health is your number one priority.

The second component of fitness is strength. Nothing beats progressive resistance training with weights to build strength. Lifting weights not only makes you strong and fit, but it also gives you self-confidence. When it comes to lifting weights, as with many things in life, slow but steady wins the race. If you try to become strong too intensely or too quickly, you'll actually become weaker, since you will likely hurt yourself. You should do some type of progressive resistance training at least three times per week.

The third component of fitness is flexibility and balance. Yoga or other stretching exercises will help you avoid that "old man" or "old lady" style of movement that is so recognizable. You should remember that stiffness is a sign of old age, and flexibility is a sign of youth. Therefore, you should do some sort of flexibility exercises several times each week.

Remember, if you are in reasonably good shape, you will not only look better, but you will feel and think better, too. You will also have more energy and more confidence. Your overall quality of life will be better in every decade of your life.

Be extraordinary, and make sure your exercise program includes the three components of fitness.

"Nothing lifts me out of a bad mood better than a hard workout on my treadmill. It never fails.
Exercise is nothing short of a miracle."

Source: Cher

Exercise Film: *Run Fatboy Run*
Distributed by Entertainment Film and New Line Cinema (UK)

(Five years after jilting his pregnant fiancée on their wedding day, out-of-shape Dennis decides to run a marathon to win her back. Description Source: IMDB)

WEEK 3:

Sleep—Start Your Day Early After a Good Night's Rest

A man went to the doctor complaining of insomnia.

The doctor gave him a thorough examination, found absolutely nothing physically wrong with him, and then told him, "Listen, if you ever expect to cure your insomnia, you just have to stop taking your troubles to bed with you."

"I know," said the man, "but I can't. My wife refuses to sleep alone."

We've all heard the expression, "The early bird catches the worm." There is a reason some of these expressions have lasted so long in human consciousness—it's because they contain seeds of truth.

It goes without saying that one trait of many ordinary people is that they are asleep when practically everybody else is up and going about their days. There are many reasons for them sleeping in, such as excessive drinking, drugs, or simply watching mindless television late into the night.

The successful are almost always up early. They get a head start on the day, rather than always playing catch-up. They face less traffic on their early drives to work. The early start gives them more time to organize their days. They are less likely to acquire the bad habits that frequently take place in the evening like mindless TV viewing, since they know they have to get up early.

However, as important as it is to get an early start, it is even more important for the vast majority of us to get a good night's rest of seven to eight hours. Sleep has many psychological and physiological benefits. In fact, getting adequate sleep can actually help you lose weight. So, if you want to get an early start, you are better off going to bed early.

If you are having trouble falling asleep, you may want to avoid eating, watching TV, or being on the computer for an hour or two before you plan to go to bed. Also, you want to make sure your sleeping area's lighting, noise level, and temperature are comfortable for sleeping. And the most important thing for you to have a good night's rest is knowing you have tried to make the world a better place and have wronged no one. Or, if it has not been your best day, at least go to bed with the intention to right those wrongs tomorrow.

Become extraordinary by getting a good night's sleep and an early start on your day.

"Early to bed and early to rise makes a [person] healthy, wealthy, and wise."
Source: Benjamin Franklin

Sleep Film: *While You Were Sleeping*
Distributed by Buena Vista Pictures

(Ticket collecting romantic pretends to be engaged to an unconscious man but can't fool his brother. Description source: IMDB)

WEEK 4:

Alcohol—Drink Responsibly, If at All

On New Year's Eve, Bill, knowing he was in no shape to drive, left his car parked and started walking home. A police officer stopped him as he was wobbling along. "What are you doing out here at four o'clock in the morning?" asked the police officer.

"I'm on my way to a lecture," answered Bill.
"And who on earth, in their right mind, is going to give a lecture at this time on New Year's Eve?" inquired the constable sarcastically.

"My wife," slurred Bill grimly.

Alcohol is a well-known social lubricant, and some say it has some health benefits when used in moderation. Moderation is the key concept in so many things, and this is true for alcohol, too. There is general agreement that drinking too much is harmful. However, the vast majority of us can drink moderate amounts to our benefit. Alcohol is a great relaxer and can help you unwind. On rare occasions, alcohol can open your mind to new insights by lowering your self-censors. And social drinking, like a good meal, can cement relationships.

However, alcohol is something you must handle very carefully and with a great deal of respect. A good rule of thumb is for you to limit your drinks at any social function so you don't say or do something you will find embarrassing the next day. You may want to use the Frank Sinatra approach to drinking, which I understand was to take a small sip of an offered drink, sit the glass down, and later move on to the next group.

Everyone has heard of extraordinary people who are heavy drinkers. However, often these people do not drink nearly as much as everyone believes; otherwise, they could never accomplish all that they have. Unfortunately, for others who do drink to excess, the drinking catches up with them, and they usually lose their extraordinary statuses.

Alcoholics, even those who don't recognize they are alcoholics, can harm themselves and the lives of those around them, including complete strangers. If you have a drinking problem, you should seek help—not only for your sake, but for your friends and family as well. A good indicator that you have a drinking problem is if your friends and family start telling you that you have a drinking problem.

Most people who drink will, on rare occasions, overdo it. Before you take your first drink, you should always have a plan for how you can get home safely in case you drink more than the legal driving limit. Perhaps you are with someone who can drive. Another option is to leave your vehicle and take a cab home, or perhaps there is a nearby hotel where you can spend the night. Is there someone you can call to pick you up? I know all this sounds like a hassel, but it is a lot less trouble than being arrested for driving while intoxicated or, worse yet, being involved in an accident.

Also, if you want to be an extraordinary host, in addition to making sure that your guests have a good time, you must also make sure they will have a safe trip home. If you know they have had too much to drink, find a place for them to stay or arrange for transportation home for them.

Be extraordinary and drink responsibly.

"I like to have a martini,
two at the very most.

After three I'm under the table,
after four I'm under my host."

Source: Dorothy Parker

Alcohol Film: *Sideways*
Distributed by Fox Searchlight Pictures

(Two men reaching middle age with not much to show but
disappointment, embark on a week long road trip through California's
wine country, just as one is about to take a trip down the aisle.
Description source: IMDB)

WEEK 5:

Clothing—Choose Appropriate Clothing

A man walks into an army surplus store and asks if they have any camouflage jackets.

"Yes, we do," replies the assistant. "But we can't find any of them."

Many people are under the mistaken impression that clothes don't matter. They tend to dress rather casually even when the circumstances call for attire that is more formal. Their poor clothing choices for attending wedding receptions, funeral services, or other formal occasions show what little attention they pay to the formalities of an occasion. Although these people may not pay attention to the conventionality, others do and will likely judge them poorly for their clothing choices.

Clothing choices reflect your self-image, and even the poorest, oldest, and heaviest among us can make a positive statement about themselves by what they choose to wear. It is surprising the look one can put together on limited funds, if one shops wisely and even more so if one has a sense of style. The older people among us can choose to look sophisticated, rather than frumpy. And, of course, those of us with a larger build can wear black and vertical-striped clothing. Clothing has the power to make you appear extraordinary, without you saying a word or doing anything.

Your choice of clothing is a form of communication. If you have a sense of style or have cultivated an image that is your signature look, you can break some of the norms of appropriate dress without reproach. For instance, many rock stars can get away with wearing jeans anywhere they go. You don't have to be subservient to fashions that may not bring forth your best physical features. However, you should be aware of society's clothing conventions so that you will have an understanding of how far you are deviating from the norm and whether or not you can pull it off.

It is sad when one shows up to work and someone says to him or her, "Oh, you must be interviewing today." People should treat every day like they are going to be interviewed and dress accordingly.

Be extraordinary by making sure your clothing choices say what you want people to say about you.

"Be in the habit of experimenting with your clothing so you don't get stuck for life with a self-image developed over the course of high school."

Source: Marilyn vos Savant

Clothing Film: *My Blue Heaven*
Distributed by Warner Bros.

(An all-too-uptight FBI agent must protect a larger-than-life mobster with a heart of gold, currently under witness protection in the suburbs. Description source: IMDB)

CHARACTER TRAITS

The Foundation for Being Extraordinary

WEEK 6:

Courage—Develop Both Physical and Mental Courage

An American general, a Russian general, and a British general are standing on the deck of a ship, watching war exercises.

The topic of discussion turns to human courage, and the Russian general boasts, "Russians are the most courageous people on Earth!"

Upon hearing that, the American challenges him. "Oh, yeah?"

The Russian says, "Sure! Here, Yuri! Jump off the deck (into the freezing Atlantic) and swim around the ship!"

Yuri jumps into the water and swims around the ship. The Russian turns around and says, "See, there's an example of courage!"

The American has to top this. He tells one of his men, "Jack, jump off the main mast into the ocean, and swim around the ship seven times!"

Jack jumps into the ocean and swims around the ship seven times. The American general says, "Now top that for courage!"

So they both turn around to the British general who has been standing around, watching these antics silently. They ask him, "What about your people?"

So the British guy calls up one of his people and says, "Trevor, jump off the mast and swim under the keel of the ship, will you, old chap?"

Trevor stares at his general.
"Let me get this right. You want me to jump off the mast."

"Yes."

"And swim under the keel."

"Yes."

"You must be daft!"

And so saying, Trevor turns around and saunters off.

Whereupon the British general turns to the other two and says, "Now there's an example of true courage!"

There is absolutely no way you can become extraordinary without courage. I'm not talking only about physical courage. Just as important, if not more so, is mental courage. You must exhibit the courage to say what needs to be said when it needs to be said. Do you find yourself holding back what you feel needs to be said out of fear of the social consequences or more tangible consequences that come from speaking one's mind?

You, the extraordinary person, know that you are as accountable for what you don't say or don't do as you are for what you say and do. To say and do nothing, waiting for someone else to act, is a sign of the ordinary. However, when you do speak out, you should do so tactfully. If you want your concerns to be better received, suggest solutions along with expressing your concerns.

It also takes courage to overcome the fear of trying something outside of your comfort zone. Often people don't try things that could make them extraordinary because they are afraid they will fail. So they let someone else step up to the task and make a name for themselves. You have to get beyond your fear of failing, or you will seldom accomplish anything extraordinary.

Also, there are those rare instances where you do need to exhibit physical courage by standing up to bullies or protecting the weaker members of society. You'll be surprised if you do this. There is a good chance that just standing up will be sufficient. Often, the reason bullies pick on the weak is because they lack courage themselves, and will back off when confronted.

By standing up to bullies, even if you don't prevail, you will enhance your reputation. If things go badly for you, think of this old saying: "A coward dies many times, whereas the brave dies but once." Hey, no one said being extraordinary was going to be easy. There is just something about being courageous that makes the impossible possible.

Be extraordinary by being courageous and making a difference.

"Fortune favors the brave."

Source: Publius Terentius Afer (a.k.a. Terence)

Courage Film: *Beowulf* with Christopher Lambert
Distributed by Dimension Films and by Miramax Films

(A sci-fi update of the famous sixth century poem. In a besieged land, Beowulf must battle against the hideous creature Grendel and his vengeance-seeking mother. Description Source: IMDB)

WEEK 7:

Self-Worth—Be Your Own Person

A man walked into a therapist's office looking very depressed. "Doc, you've got to help me. I can't go on like this."

"What's the problem?" the doctor inquired.

"Well, I'm thirty-five years old, and I still have no luck with the ladies. No matter how hard I try, I just seem to scare them away."

"My friend, this is not a serious problem. You just need to work on your self-esteem. Each morning, I want you to get up and run to the bathroom mirror. Tell yourself that you are a good person, a fun person, and an attractive person. But say it with real conviction. Within a week you'll have women buzzing all around you."

The man seemed content with this advice and walked out of the office a bit excited. Three weeks later, he returned with the same downtrodden expression on his face.

"Didn't my advice work?" asked the doctor.

"It worked all right. For the past several weeks I've enjoyed some of the best moments in my life with the most fabulous-looking women."

"So, what's your problem?"
"I don't have a problem," the man replied. "My wife does."

Ordinary people do more to keep themselves ordinary than other people or events could ever do. When opportunity knocks, the ordinary person tends not to open that door. They think of one reason after another why they are not worthy of the opportunity or of the consequences should they fail. You can just listen to their self-deprecating speeches and know they don't believe in themselves or even expect fair treatment. When others compliment them, rather than simply saying thank you, they often say something to negate the compliment given to them.

Extraordinary people believe in themselves and their self-talk plays a major role in creating and maintaining that belief. When talking about themselves to others, they never put themselves down even to be humorous. They develop courage slowly by taking on small fears initially, and as their confidence slowly grows, they tackle greater fears. In time, they develop the courage to believe in themselves and to live their own lives by standing up to others who try to force them to be someone they are not.

Another area where ordinary people often differ from extraordinary people is that ordinary people tend to undervalue their goods and services and either give them away or sell them for far less than the going rate. They ask for so little, and that is what they receive. It takes confidence and courage to ask for a fair price for your goods and services. If you don't believe in the value of your goods and services, then who will?

Be extraordinary by believing in yourself and being your own person.

"If you think you can do a thing
or if you think you can't,
either way, you are right."

Source: Henry Ford

Self-Worth Film: *Great Expectations* with Gwyneth Paltrow
Distributed by Warner Bros.

(Modernization of Charles Dickens classic story finds the hapless
Finn as a painter in New York pursuing his unrequited and haughty
childhood love. Description source: IMDB)

WEEK 8:

Action—Take Some Meaningful Action Daily to Make Your Dreams Come True

There are five frogs on a log.
One decides to jump off.
How many are left?
Five—because deciding isn't doing.

Any time you are going to make an important decision, it is always a good idea to sleep on it and see if things look the same way as they did the day before. However, sleeping on a decision to obtain a clearheaded perspective is far from avoiding making a decision.

Many ordinary people simply can't bring themselves to take action; instead, they continue to seek information. The name of this type of behavior is "paralysis by analysis." The extent of information about anything can be practically unlimited, and it is subject to the law of diminishing returns. You have to ask yourself if gathering still more information will cause you to change your decision. If additional information will not cause you to act differently, why bother?

You must realize that postponing a decision is a decision—it is the decision to not take action. And, when you are finally ready to make a decision and take action, often the opportunity has passed you by. By not doing anything, you have let events or other people take control. You cannot be like this and be extraordinary. After a lifetime, most people regret the things they didn't do more than the things that they did.

Some decisions are simply inconsequential, like which card to play in a casual game of cards or what to order in a restaurant that you have been to many times. However, these moments help you to develop the habit of being decisive. If you can't be decisive when it comes to inconsequential decisions, how will you ever make a decision on important matters?

In addition, you should remember that activity is not the same as accomplishment. It is easy for people to be extremely busy and fool themselves into thinking they are accomplishing something. Yes, you need to take action, but that action needs to be meaningful and not simply activity.

Be extraordinary, and take some meaningful action every day, regardless of how small, to make your dreams come true and your life extraordinary.

The moment one definitely commits oneself, then providence moves, too.

All sorts of things occur to help one.

A whole stream of events issues from the decision, raising in one's favor all manner of unforeseen incidents and meetings and material assistance which no person could have dreamed would come their way.

"Whatever you can do or dream you can, begin it!"

"Boldness has genius, power, and magic in it."

Source: Goethe

Action Film: *Kick-Ass*
Distributed by Universal Pictures (International), Lionsgate
(North America) and Alliance Films (Canada)

(Dave Lizewski is an unnoticed high school student and comic book
fan who one day decides to become a super-hero, even though he has
no powers, training or meaningful reason to do so.
Description source: IMDB)

WEEK 9:

Visualization—In Your Mind's Eye, See Yourself as Extraordinary

Two elderly couples were enjoying friendly conversation when one of the men asked the other, "Fred, how was the memory clinic you went to last month?"

"Outstanding," Fred replied. "They taught us all the latest psychological techniques—visualization, association—it made a huge difference for me."

"That's great! What was the name of the clinic?"

Fred went blank. He thought and thought, but couldn't remember. Then a smile broke across his face and he asked, "What do you call that red flower with the long stem and thorns?"

"You mean a rose?"

"Yes, that's it!" He turned to his wife. "Rose, what was the name of that clinic?"

Practically all successful athletes practice visualization. They spend time visualizing themselves lifting huge weights, crossing the finishing line, hitting the ball out of the park, and so on. Many business executives have also used visualization to help them land an important client or succeed in an interview. Meditation is also useful in assisting you in your efforts to become extraordinary.

If you can't imagine something, then it is unlikely it will happen. Many ordinary people aren't even aware of the practice of visualization, or they can't visualize themselves as anything other than ordinary. They are completely comfortable with their roles of being ordinary and very uncomfortable with the thought of being extraordinary.

If you want to become extraordinary, you have to spend time visualizing yourself as extraordinary. You have to see yourself as someone who already possesses the traits described in this book. The more specifically you visualize, the better.

Be extraordinary by seeing yourself in your imagination as extraordinary.

"Imagination is more important than knowledge."

Source: Albert Einstein

Visualization Film: *Café*
Distributed by Nationlight Productions

(A good-hearted musician struggles to find a way to tell his beautiful barista coworker that he loves her, despite the fact that she is in a relationship. Meanwhile, regulars and customers at the café where they work have their own problems and encounters. A police officer keeps his eye on his wayward cousin, who owes money to a charismatic dealer, and a married man contemplates his relationship with a good-looking new acquaintance. However, one customer believes he is in fact the main character in a computer simulation of modern life, set in the microcosm of the café, all designed by a young girl. Description source: Wikipedia)

WEEK 10:

Optimism—Never Lose Hope

Three friends had a good friend named Joe, and he was, by nature, an eternal optimist.

At every bad situation, he would always say, "It could have been worse."

His friends hated that quality about him, so they came up with a story so horrible that not even Joe could come up with a bright side.

The next day, only two of his friends showed up for a golf date.

Joe asked, "Where's Gary?"

And one of his friends said, "Didn't you hear? Yesterday, Gary found his wife in bed with another man, shot them both, and then turned the gun on himself."

Joe says, 'Well it could have been worse."

Both his friends said, "How could it be worse? Your best friend just killed himself!"

Joe replies, "If it had happened two days ago, I'd be dead now!"

One of the earmarks of many ordinary people is negativity. Ordinary people tend to dwell on all the reasons their dreams cannot come true, and they will be glad to explain in detail why your dreams also cannot come true. Many ordinary people are anything other than uplifting, and interacting with them can cause you to feel less optimistic.

Unlike ordinary people, extraordinary people are optimistic. They believe their dreams will come true, and they even believe the dreams of others will come true. If you are optimistic and encouraging to others, people will like being around you and think well of you. A positive and upbeat attitude rubs off on everyone around you, which helps him or her view you as an extraordinary person.

All extraordinary people encounter setbacks in the pursuit of their objectives. Rather than becoming depressed, these extraordinary people do not give up. Yes, they may reassess their goals to determine if those goals are worthy of their continued efforts, and if they still feel the goals are worthy ones, they will work through the setbacks to achieve them.

Be extraordinary by encouraging others to pursue their dreams, and remain optimistic about achieving your own dreams.

"It will be all right in the end, and if it isn't all right,
it is not yet the end."

Source: The Best Exotic Marigold Hotel

Optimism Film: *Salmon Fishing in the Yemen*
Distributed by Lionsgate (UK) and CBS Films (USA)

(A fisheries expert is approached by a consultant to help realize a sheik's vision of bringing the sport of fly-fishing to the desert and embarks on an upstream journey of faith and fish to prove the impossible possible.
Description source: IMDB)

WEEK 11:

Limitations—Extremes Are Harmful

An Irishman is stumbling through the woods, very drunk, when he comes upon a preacher baptizing people in the river.

The preacher turns around and is almost overcome by the smell of alcohol on the Irishman, whereupon he asks, "Are you ready to find Jesus?"

The Irishman shouts, "Yes, I am."

So the preacher grabs him and dunks him in the water.

He pulls him back and asks, "Brother, have you found Jesus?"

The Irishman replies, "No, I haven't found Jesus!"

The preacher, shocked at the answer, dunks him again but for a little longer.

He again pulls him out of the water and asks, "Have you found Jesus, my brother?"

The Irishman answers, "No, I haven't found Jesus!"

By this time, the preacher is at his wits end and dunks the Irishman again—but this time holds him down for about thirty seconds, and when he begins kicking his arms and legs about, the preacher pulls him up.
The preacher again asks the Irishman, "For the love of God, have you found Jesus?"

The Irishman staggers upright, wipes his eyes, coughs up a bit of water, catches his breath, and says to the preacher,

"Are you sure this is where he fell in?"

Ordinary people tend to get excited about something and then over-do it without any awareness of their limitations. For instance, if they try to be strong, they work out so much and so hard that they end up injuring themselves and making themselves weaker. They don't seem to realize that, yes, to get strong they need to challenge themselves, but not to the extent of exceeding their natural limitations.

The same holds true for those trying to become attractive who overdo their efforts to the point that they become unattractive. We have all seen the woman who simply has had too much plastic surgery. Or perhaps we have seen a guy who is trying hard to look cool by wearing a lot of bling and ends up looking like a fool. Or how about the guy who starts to loosen up a bit with a drink or two, but then thinks more will make him even more charming, and instead makes himself obnoxious. All these people would be better off to accept their natural limitations and simply make the most of what they have without going to extremes.

I'm not saying that you should practice moderation in everything you do, since that could lead to a long and boring life. The extraordinary person goes up to the edge of the cliff, but is smart enough not to go over the edge.

"When something reaches its extreme, it changes to the opposite."

Source: Deng Ming-Dao

Moderation Film: *Magnum Force*
Distributed by Warner Bros.

(Dirty Harry is on the trail of vigilante cops who are not above going
beyond the law to kill the city's undesirables. Description source:
IMDB)

WEEK 12:

Endurance—If Your Goal Is Worthy, Don't Give Up

A man was driving down the road one rainy day when his car suddenly broke down in front of a small monastery. To escape the rain, he walked up to the monastery and knocked on the door.

The head monk answered the door and said, "Ah, hello. How may I help you?"

"Um, hello," the man replied. "My car broke down, and I was wondering if you had a phone or something for me to call for help."

"Well," the head monk said, "We do not have any phones here; however, we can send one of our monks to the city and get you help. In the meantime, you are allowed to stay here in the monastery."

The man thanked the head monk and went inside. The other monks graciously accepted him as one of their own. They fed him, provided him with a bath, and gave him his own little bed. Then, later that night, the man heard a noise. It was a sound unlike anything he had ever heard before. He stayed up all night, tossing and turning, trying to think of what it could be.

The next morning, he walked up to the head monk and said, "Hello, I was wondering if I could ask you a question."

"Yes," the head monk said. "What is it you would like to know?"

"Well, you see," the man said, "yesterday I heard a strange noise, and I was wondering if you knew what it was."

"Oh, I'm sorry," the head monk said in reply. "I cannot tell you, for you are not a monk."

"Well, then how do I become a monk?" the man asked, desperate to find out what the beautiful noise was.

"There is a test you must take," the head monk answered. "You must go all around the world, count all the blades of grass and all the grains of sand, and then come back here."

The man spent many years traveling the world, seeking out the answer to the monks' test of faith, endurance, and bravery, with the yearning to find out about the noise pushing him forward.

Finally, ten years later, the man returned to the monastery. The head monk greeted him and led him to a small room, filled with other monks. "Now," the head monk said, "how many blades of grass and grains of sand are there?"

The man replied, "By design, the world is in a state of perpetual change. Only God knows what you ask. All a man can know is himself, and only then if he is honest and reflective and willing to strip away self-deception."

The monks shouted with glee. They congratulated him, gave him gifts, and then the head monk handed him a small golden key.

"Take this," he said. "There is a small golden door on the other side of the monastery. This is the key to that door."

The man went and unlocked the door. Behind it was a silver door, with a silver key in it. Behind that door was a ruby door, and behind that, a diamond door. The man stepped through many doors. Through platinum, sapphire, iron, steel, and finally, he came to a plain, wooden door, with a plain wooden key.

He turned the key, and upon opening the door just a crack, he heard the noise again. "How beautiful," he thought to himself. He then thrust the door open and saw what it was that had made the noise. He fell to his knees in awe of what it was that had produced the amazing, seductive sound...

But, of course, I cannot tell you what it was, for you are not a monk.

Endurance is another trait that clearly separates the extraordinary people from ordinary people.

The extraordinary people find it in themselves to endure and to keep on trying regardless of how hopeless their situations seem or how many approaches they have tried. Whereas, ordinary people live by the saying, "If at first you don't succeed, try something else." If you are sure your goal is worthy, then you should keep trying and never give up.

However, failure and disappointment sometimes are nature's way of protecting you from yourself. There is an ancient Chinese curse that says, "May your every wish be granted."

Life always presents you with ups and downs. The downs are life's way of making sure you appreciate the ups, and sometimes the downs are life's way of telling you that perhaps you should rethink your goal. You should understand that difficult times have their purposes.

Be extraordinary, and if you are sure your goal is worthy, don't give up—endure.

"One of these days, you will not be able to do this. Today isn't that day!"

Source: Sign in the crowd at the 2011 Chicago
Rock 'n' Roll Half Marathon

Endurance Film: *Rocky*
Distributed by United Artists

(Rocky Balboa, a small-time boxer gets a supremely rare chance to
fight the heavy-weight champion, Apollo Creed, in a bout in which he
strives to go the distance for his self-respect.
Description source: IMDB)

WEEK 13:

Anger—Actions Speak Louder than Words

A cowboy rode into town and stopped at a saloon for a drink. Unfortunately, the locals always had a habit of picking on strangers, which he was. The cowboy found his horse missing after he finished his drink.

He went back into the bar, handily flipped his gun into the air, caught it above his head without even looking, and fired a shot into the ceiling. "Which one of you sidewinders stole my horse?" he yelled with surprising forcefulness.

No one answered. "All right. I'm gonna have another beer, and if my horse ain't back outside by the time I finish, I'm gonna do what I done in Texas! And I don't like to have to do what I done in Texas!"

Some of the locals shifted restlessly. The man, true to his word, had another beer, walked outside, and his horse had been returned to the post. He saddled up and started to ride out of town.

The bartender wandered out of the bar and asked, "Say partner, before you go…what happened in Texas?"

The cowboy turned back and said, "I had to walk home."

Fighters knows that the surest way to beat their opponents is to make them angry so that their thinking shuts down, leaving them vulnerable. This tactic will work in any situation where people are disagreeing with one another and not just in physical contests.

You can just look at the faces of angry people and know their thinking has shut down by how unpleasant their faces have become. Extraordinary people also feel anger, but they do their best not to let it show in their facial expressions.

Have you ever listened to the language of angry people? You will notice that their speech is peppered with swear words. Possibly, the ordinary person uses such words to appear powerful; however, it is more likely a sign of weakness. You can bet that more often than not, angry people say things they quickly regret, whereas extraordinary people say very little until they have regained their composure, sometimes even taking a few deep breaths before speaking. Consequently, they rarely regret their words. This tactic can also be unsettling to the other parties involved since we have all heard the old saying, "Don't get angry, get even."

Extraordinary people don't take the bait when someone intentionally or unintentionally angers them. As for the individuals who routinely anger them, extraordinary people do their best to limit contact with these individuals or remain on guard when around them. On the other hand, perhaps it isn't individuals, but instead just certain situations or topics of discussion that make people angry. Whatever it is, extraordinary people try to use their feelings of anger as learning opportunities.

Be extraordinary, and don't let anger control you.

"Speak softly, and carry a big stick."

Source: Teddy Roosevelt

Anger Film: *Analyze This*
Distributed by Warner Bros. and Roadshow Entertainment (Australia and New Zealand)

(A comedy about a psychiatrist whose number one patient is an insecure mob boss. Description source: IMDB)

WEEK 14:

Instinct—Pay Attention to Your Instincts

A mama skunk, a daddy skunk and a baby skunk
became lost in the woods.
"My instincts," said the mama skunk, "tell me to go left."
The daddy skunk shook his head, "My instincts," he said,
"tell me to go right."
The baby skunk looked at them both a bit puzzled, and said, "My end
stinks. But it doesn't tell me anything."

Most of us live in a world of rules, and often ordinary people are not even aware of the rules governing their thinking. Societies script us to think this or that and to override our natural instincts. Rules and guidelines are important for an orderly society, but sometimes you need to follow your instincts and do the right thing rather than "doing things right." For example, if you want to make a breakthrough in some area, you need to follow your instincts. Remember, there was a time when conventional wisdom said the world was flat and ordinary people of that time did not question that statement.

Extraordinary people pay attention to their instincts. Instincts are like internal beacons, keeping us from harm or showing us the way forward. They have permitted the human race to survive in its beginnings and continue to do so even today. How many times have you done something and later said, "I knew I should not have done that"? This happens when you don't trust your instincts.

Be extraordinary, and pay attention to your instincts.

"The heart has reasons that reason will never know."
Source: Blaise Pascal

Instinct Film: *Ruby Sparks*
Distributed by Fox Searchlight Pictures

(A novelist struggling with writer's block finds romance in a most unusual way: by creating a female character he thinks will love him, then willing her into existence. Description source: IMDB)

WEEK 15:

Promises—Keep Them

A dying man gives an envelope containing twenty-five thousand dollars in cash to each of his best friends (a lawyer, a doctor, and a clergyman), with instructions that the cash is to be placed in his coffin.

A week later, the man dies and the friends each place an envelope in the coffin. Several months later, the clergyman confesses that he only put $10,000 in the envelope and sent the rest to a mission in South America.

The doctor confesses that his envelope had only $8,000 because he donated to a medical charity.

The lawyer is outraged. "I am the only one who kept my promise to our dying friend. I want you both to know that the envelope I placed in the coffin contained my own personal check for the entire $25,000."

The word of many ordinary people means very little. They make commitments with little regard for actually carrying them out. They don't own enough of themselves to say no, so they tend to say yes to everything and actually do very little. Every time you fail to carry out a promise or commitment, your reputation suffers.

Extraordinary people keep their promises, perhaps because they make so few of them. One of the best ways for you to keep a promise is not to make one. You should be very reluctant about agreeing to do anything, because your promises mean something. They mean you will carry them out without fail. Before you promise anything, even to yourself, you must be certain of two things. First, that what you have promised is something you really want to do. Second, that what you have promised is actually something that you can do.

Be extraordinary, and keep your promises to others as well as to yourself.

"The best way to keep one's word is not to give it."

Source: Napoleon Bonaparte

Promises Film: *Broken Flowers*
Distributed by Focus Features

(As the extremely withdrawn Don Johnston is dumped by his latest woman, he receives an anonymous letter from a former lover informing him that he has a son who may be looking for him. A freelance sleuth neighbor moves Don to embark on a cross-country search for his old flames in search of answers. Description source: IMDB)

WEEK 16:

Jealousy—Avoid

Not that my wife is the jealous type or anything, but one day at work, I had taken my temporary secretary to lunch in gratitude for an outstanding job she did on a very difficult project.

As luck would have it, my wife was waiting in the office for my return.

The temporary secretary, who was an attractive young woman said, "Oh, Mrs. Moore, I'm so happy to meet you. I'm your husband's temporary secretary."

My wife quickly replied, "Oh? Really? Were you?"

There are always going to be people who you believe are better than you are. Ordinary people are envious of what other people have and the positions they hold, plus numerous other things. Therefore, many ordinary people can never offer a sincere compliment. They view the world as a lump-sum game, and if someone has more of something, it means they have less of it and cannot be glad about others' good fortunes.

You must be just the opposite of the ordinary person. You must be quick with a compliment, recognize the achievements of others, and make it clear that you are glad about the good fortunes of others.

Being envious can keep you from becoming extraordinary because no matter how hard you try, your envy will eventually show in one way or another. The extraordinary person truly appreciates the successes, skills, accomplishments, and good fortunes of others. In the rare instances where extraordinary people start to feel envy, they make changes in their own lives to satisfy the desires causing their feelings of envy.

Be extraordinary by giving sincere compliments, and guard against being jealous or envious.

"Wanting a thing is often more desirable than having a thing; it is not logical, but it is often true."

Source: Spock

Jealousy Film: *Amadeus*

(The incredible story of Wolfgang Amadeus Mozart, told by his peer and secret rival Antonio Salieri—now confined to an insane asylum. Description source: IMDB)

WEEK 17:

Truthfulness—Be Meticulous About Telling the Truth,
But Don't Be Cruel About It

A father bought a lie detector robot that slaps people when they lie.
He decided to test it at dinner one night.
The father asked his son what he did that day. The son said, "I did some
schoolwork."
The robot slapped the son.
The son said, "OK, OK. I was at a friend's house watching movies."
Dad asked, "What movie did you watch?" The son said, "*Toy Story.*"
The robot slapped the son.
The son said, "OK, OK. We were watching porn."
Dad said, "What? At your age I didn't even know what porn was!"
The robot slapped the father.
Mom laughed and said, "Well he certainly is your son!"
The robot slapped the mother!
P.S. Robot for Sale

Often, ordinary people tend to be very unreliable reporters at best. Under some circumstances, ordinary people will lie if they feel the truth will not be well received or put them in a bad light. At other times, they will only tell a portion of the story, perhaps without even realizing that not giving all the details is another form of untruthfulness. They may not be directly telling a lie, but they are still misleading someone by not telling the full and complete truth. One who misleads another is no nobler than the person who is deliberately lying. If you lie or tell half-truths, people will eventually find you out and your credibility will be lost.

Extraordinary people tend to be meticulous in telling the truth even about unimportant matters. If you are not positive of the facts, you should always point out that you "believe" or you have "heard" something and that you aren't certain of the facts. Consequently, you will earn a reputation for truthfulness and credibility.

However, your devotion to telling the truth is not a license to be unkind or to cause harm to others. You may find it better simply to not say anything than to be cruel under the banner of truthfulness. If you are in a situation where you must give your opinion, perhaps you can carefully use humor to soften your message—or perhaps you have found yourself in one of those rare times where a lie may be preferable to the truth. The extraordinary person knows there are exceptions to every rule.

Be extraordinary by being meticulous about telling the truth, but don't use truthfulness as an excuse to be cruel.

"Humor is a rubber sword—it allows you to make a point without drawing blood."

Source: Mary Hirsch

Truthfulness Film: *Liar Liar*
Distributed by Universal Pictures

(A fast-track lawyer can't lie for twenty-four hours due to his son's birthday wish after the lawyer turns his son down for the last time. Description source: IMDB)

WEEK 18:

Detachment—Develop a Healthy Detachment to Your Objects and Relationships

A law professor asked the students what they would do, as a judge, if the plaintiff gave them a ten-thousand-dollar bribe, and the defendant gave them a twenty-thousand-dollar bribe.

None of the students gave the correct answer.

The law professor told the students they should return ten thousand dollars to the defendant and decide the case on its merits.

We come into the world with nothing, and each of us will go out the same way. Have you ever watched what happens to the belongings of an older person who dies? There is a lesson in seeing their treasures put to the curb or sold in a garage sale, with people haggling over the few cents being asked for these items.

As for the people who come into our lives, well, they are often with us only for a while, and then they are gone. There is very little we can do to stop this from occurring. Some move away, some die, some change jobs, some get married, and others have children; all these situations will change their relationships with you. Many ordinary people desperately try to cling to material objects and people, even when it is clearly time to let them go. Some examples of things and people that one should let go of are a favorite vase that is cracked and no longer holds water or a key team member who has accepted a better job. For the vase, perhaps taking a photo may be a better option than storing something that no longer functions. As for the team member, if you really appreciate the person, simply wish him or her well.

Extraordinary people recognize the impermanence of all things. They appreciate their material possessions and their relationships, yet they will freely let them go when it is time for them to go.

It is especially important to have a detached attitude when you are making decisions. It is so easy to make a bad decision based on what you want to see rather than seeing what is really there. A better approach is for you to detach your emotions from important decisions and balance logic with what your heart tells you afterward.

Be extraordinary, and develop a healthy detachment with your objects and your relationships.

"Desperation is the worst cologne."

Source: Chris Rock

Detachment Film: *Somebody Up There Likes Me*
Distributed by Tribeca Film

(The film skips through 35 years in the life of Max Youngman, following him through his courtship and marriage to Lyla, also the object of affection for his best friend Sal. Never seeming to age, Max and the adult characters closest to him stumble in and out of comically misguided relationships and happenstances that are seamlessly woven together by animated vignettes provided by Bob Sabiston. Description source: Wikipedia)

WEEK 19:

Change—Embrace All Changes for the Opportunities They Can Provide

John received a parrot as a gift; the problem was that the parrot had a bad attitude and an even worse vocabulary. Every word out of the bird's mouth was rude, obnoxious, and laced with profanity. John tried and tried to change the bird's attitude by consistently saying only polite words, playing soft music, and anything else he could think of to "clean up" the bird's vocabulary, but to no avail.

John, fed up, yelled at the parrot. The parrot yelled back. John shook the parrot and the parrot got angrier and even ruder. In desperation, John threw up his hands, grabbed the bird, and put him in the freezer. For a few minutes, the parrot squawked and kicked. Then suddenly, there was total quiet.

Fearing that he'd killed the parrot, John quickly opened the door to the freezer. The parrot calmly stepped out onto John's outstretched arm and said, "I believe I may have offended you with my rude language and actions. I am sincerely remorseful for my inappropriate transgressions, and I fully intend to do everything I can to correct my rude and unforgivable behavior."

John was stunned at the change in the bird's attitude. As he was about to ask the parrot what had made such a dramatic change in his behavior, the bird said, "May I ask what the chicken did?"

Change is inevitable; it will come. Nothing stays the same. There will be changes to your world, to your employment, to your relationships, and to your body, and you will have no choice in the matter. What you will have is the choice of how you react to those changes.

Being uncomfortable with flexibility is a sign of aging and eventual demise, whether we are talking about nature, organizations, or our own bodies. The more rigid we become, the closer we are to extinction. Ordinary people tend to repeat the same things in the fruitless hope of receiving different results, especially if what they are repeating worked in a prior situation. In contrast, the extraordinary person is able to quickly recognize that what worked in the prior situation will not work in the current situation.

I'm not saying you should like change. Those who say they like change are typically the authors of that change or are fooling themselves or trying to fool you. Moreover, all of us have been victims of change for change's sake; nevertheless, one still needs to adapt. Unfortunately, or perhaps fortunately, nothing stays the same.

We all experience major changes. If you do not adjust to these changes, you will be sorry. That is certain. However, change is also where major opportunities reside.

We all experience smaller, minor changes practically every day, too. Our failure to recognize or adjust to these minor changes generally results in little harm to us. However, extraordinary people tend to recognize these small changes and make adjustments so that little by little, making adjustments to change becomes second nature to them.

Be extraordinary, and look for the opportunities provided by both small and major changes.

"A [person] is born gentle and weak.

At [one's] death [one is] hard and stiff.

Green plants are tender and filled with sap.
At their death, they are withered and dry.

Therefore, the stiff and unbending is the disciple of death.

The gentle and yielding is the disciple of life.

Thus, an army without flexibility never wins a battle.

A tree that is unbending is easily broken."

Source: Lao Tzu

Change Film: *Don't Tempt Me*
Distributed by Casa Nova Films

(Two angels, one from the heaven and one from the hell, come to earth
to save the soul of a boxer. Description source: IMDB)

WEEK 20:

Celebrate—Your Own Successes, and Especially the Successes of Your Friends

Upon dying, the pope goes to heaven where he meets a reception committee. They tell the pope that he can enjoy any of the many recreations available.

He decides that he wants to read all of the ancient original texts of the holy Scriptures and spends the next eon learning the languages. After becoming a linguistic master, he sits down in the library and begins to read every version of the Bible, working back from the most recent, "Easy Reading," to the original.

All of a sudden, there is a scream in the library. The angels come running to him, only to find the pope huddled in a chair, crying to himself, and muttering, "An *R*! They left out the *R*."

God takes him aside, offering comfort, and asks him what the problem is. After collecting his wits, the pope sobs again, "It's the letter *R*...the word was supposed to be *celebrate*."

Extraordinary people always seem to be celebrating something. We can say to ourselves, "These people have a lot to celebrate, but what does an ordinary person like me have to celebrate?" Perhaps extraordinary people are extraordinary *because* they celebrate, and not that they celebrate because they are extraordinary. They not only celebrate their major accomplishments, but also their small accomplishments. Their habit of celebrating serves as motivation.

But what really makes them extraordinary is that they are every bit as quick, if not quicker, to celebrate the large and even the small accomplishments of their friends and team members before their own.

National holidays are a good reason to celebrate. Of course, many ordinary people celebrate national holidays, so the extraordinary person often also celebrates some of the less-celebrated holidays, such as Groundhog Day or Martin Luther King Jr. Day.

And, of course, there are always the personal holidays, such as birthdays and anniversaries. It is even better to celebrate the birthdays and anniversaries of your friends, especially those friends who don't make a big deal of these milestones.

Be extraordinary, and look for opportunities celebrate.

"The more you praise and celebrate your life,
the more there is in life to celebrate."

Source: Oprah Winfrey

Celebrate Film: *Dinner for Schmucks*
Distributed by Paramount Pictures

(When he finds out that his work superiors host a dinner celebrating
the idiocy of their guests, a rising executive questions it when he's
invited, just as he befriends a man who would be the perfect guest.
Description source: IMDB)

WEEK 21:

Forgettaboutit—Forgive All, but Have a Good Memory

Attorney: This myasthenia gravis, does it affect your memory at all?

Witness: Yes.

Attorney: And in what ways does it affect your memory?

Witness: I forget.

Attorney: You forget? Can you give us an example of something you forgot?

Ordinary people tend to hold on to their anger or their disappointment. They do not easily offer forgiveness or even forget about the wrongs they have experienced. They appear to live by that old saying, "If a person can't hold a grudge forever, it just shows that person has no character." This old saying is clearly false and harmful.

Extraordinary people forgive wrongs or injustices done to them, and if that isn't possible, they at least try to forget so they can move forward with their lives. Sometimes the extraordinary person is even able to forge a new and stronger bond with the people who have wronged them. Even if the offenders refuse to acknowledge their wrongs, you should forgive them—not for their sake but for your own.

Although it is useful for people to forgive a wrong, or at least to forget it, that does not mean they will be fools in their future dealings with offending people. There is another old saying that is clearly true: Fool me once, shame on you. Fool me twice, shame on me.

Be extraordinary, and forgive all offenders, but watch your future dealings with these people.

"God, grant me the serenity to accept the things I cannot change,
courage to change the things I can,
and the wisdom to know the difference."

Source: Serenity Prayer

Forgettaboutit Film: *The Descendants*
Distributed by Fox Searchlight Pictures

(A land baron tries to reconnect with his two daughters after his wife is
seriously injured in a boating accident. Description source: IMDB)

WEEK 22:

Discard—Reduce Clutter in Your Life

A young executive was leaving the office late one evening when he found the CEO standing in front of a shredder with a piece of paper in his hand.

"Listen," said the CEO, "this is a very sensitive and important document here, and my secretary has gone for the night. Can you make this thing work?"

"Certainly," said the young executive. He turned the machine on, inserted the paper, and pressed the start button.

"Excellent, excellent!" said the CEO as his paper disappeared inside the machine.
"I just need one copy."

Less is more. You've heard it many times, and that is because it is true. Be lean and retain only what you need in your life as it is today. If something from the past inspires you today, then keep it. However, if it is just a memory, it's time for you to discard it and move on to making new memories.

Clutter is the enemy of extraordinary people. Extraordinary people are quick to discard things and ideas that no longer serve a purpose. Sometimes people even have to let go of former friends because they are holding them back from becoming extraordinary. For instance, the young person from a poor neighborhood who is trying to obtain a college education, whose friends start making fun of him. You have to realize that there are people who will feel you are betraying them as you work toward creating your dream life, and they will try to undermine your efforts.

As for material things, if you are having a hard time parting with something for sentimental reasons, take a picture of the object and then pass the object on to someone that may actually have a use for it. Extraordinary people also don't hang on to things thinking that someday they may prove useful. Besides, even if people do this, they probably will not be able to find the object when they do need it because of all the other clutter.

One of the biggest sources of clutter is paper. You can file paper away, but often it is still clutter. The next time you file something, write the date that you filed it on the item, and then write the date the next time you make use of that filed item.

We are also entering the age of electronic clutter. We all know people who can't seem to manage their e-mails or their voice mail. Clutter is clutter, regardless of its form, and clutter is always the enemy of extraordinary people.

A good practice is that each day, as you move through your life, you will see something that no longer serves you—discard it. Simplify your life so you can be quick and agile.

A number of ordinary people are hoarders. They hang on to everything, including relationships that no longer serve them, jobs that no longer inspire them, and belief systems that are no longer in synch with the modern world we live in.

Don't be held prisoner by your stuff. Be extraordinary by discarding daily.

[When] clearing out clutter, ask [yourself],

"Does this look like it belongs to the person I want to be?"

Source: "This Year I Will" by MJ Ryan

Discard Film: *Everything Must Go*

(When an alcoholic relapses, causing him to lose his wife and his job, he holds a yard sale on his front lawn in an attempt to start over. A new neighbor might be the key to his return to form. Description source: IMDB)

WEEK 23:

Money—Save 10 Percent of What You Earn

A preacher one Sunday announced to his congregation,
"I have good news and bad news."

The preacher then said, "The good news is, we have enough money to
pay for our new building program."

He then added, "The bad news is, it's still out there in your pockets."

There is an old saying that money cannot buy happiness. Over a certain minimum amount, additional money does not lead to additional happiness. The things extra money buys come with additional responsibility and problems. There may be some truth to the saying, "The two best days for a boat owner are the day he buys the boat and the day he sells it." Nevertheless, there is no doubt that one requires a certain minimum amount of money to have a chance at happiness. However, additional money alone will not make you extraordinary. What can make you extraordinary is how you use that additional money.

One way for you to acquire sufficient money to permit you to be happy and extraordinary is simply for you to earn a lot of money; however, it is surprising how many people who earn a lot of money are way over their heads in debt. Too often, those making a lot of money spend even more money. You may want to remember the saying, "If you want to know what someone values, look where they spend their money."

Another, perhaps surer, way to have an adequate supply of money is by saving. Saving is an activity that clearly separates ordinary people from the extraordinary. Many ordinary people save nothing. They spend money as fast as they get it. If they don't have money, they live on credit, which is really mortgaging their futures.

It is difficult for the poor to be noble unless they are a monk or choose that lifestyle for philosophical reasons. If one does not have a reasonable amount of money put away, it can be a challenge to maintain one's honor. How many people have to do something they consider dishonorable at work because they simply cannot afford to quit their jobs because they failed to put away some "I quit" money? In addition, without adequate money, you cannot be generous and help those you wish to help.

Extraordinary people always save at least 10 percent of everything they make. It is easy for them to do that because they live below their means. They don't try to impress others with their consumption. Still, they are impressive because they never had to sell their honor due to debt and because they could afford to be generous.

The following is something I came across early in life, and I have never forgotten it. I read that out of one hundred young people of twenty-five years of age, at sixty-five:

Thirty-six have died,

One is rich,

Four are independent,

Five are working, and

Fifty-four are dependent.

Be extraordinary by developing the habit of always saving at least 10 percent of everything you earn.

"Money is a good servant, but a bad master."

Source: Henry Bohn

Money Film: *Jerry Maguire*
Distributed by TriStar Pictures

(When a sports agent has a moral epiphany and is fired for expressing it, he decides to put his new philosophy to the test as an independent with the only athlete who stays with him. Description source: IMDB)

WEEK 24:

Ask—People Aren't Mind Readers, Politely Ask for What You Want

Attorney: Doctor, before you performed the autopsy, did you check for a pulse?

Witness: No.

Attorney: Did you check for blood pressure?

Witness: No.

Attorney: Did you check for breathing?

Witness: No.

Attorney: So, then it is possible that the patient was alive when you began the autopsy?

Witness: No.

Attorney: How can you be so sure, Doctor?

Witness: Because his brain was sitting on my desk in a jar.

Attorney: I see. But could the patient still have been alive, nevertheless?

Witness: Yes, it is possible that he could have been alive and practicing law.

Extraordinary people aren't afraid to ask for what they want. Of course, they don't ask in a threatening or irritating way, but they do ask. Ordinary people, on the other hand, are often afraid to ask for what they want and instead hope that someone will recognize their need and satisfy it. Ordinary people may even drop tiny hints about what they want, thinking this is asking, but it isn't, and it is very likely that those hints will go unnoticed.

What is the worst thing that can happen if you ask for something? Probably the worst thing is that you will receive a negative answer and perhaps feel a little embarrassed. At least by asking, you are making sure the person you are asking knows what you want. By making sure they know what you want, you have dramatically increased the odds of eventually getting what you want or at least knowing you aren't going to get it from that person. With that valuable piece of information, you can change your desires or move on to where your desires are more likely to be satisfied.

Additionally, before you ask for something, you may want to double check to make sure you are worthy of what you want. If you feel you aren't, most likely the person you are asking will also feel that way. Therefore, if you feel you aren't worthy, you have some work to do before you ask.

Be extraordinary by having the courage to ask politely for what you want and to gracefully accept a negative response.

"If you don't ask, you don't get."

Source: Mahatma Gandhi

Ask Film: *I Love You, Beth Cooper*

(A nerdy valedictorian proclaims his love for the hottest and most popular girl in school—Beth Cooper—during his graduation speech. Much to his surprise, Beth shows up at his door that very night and decides to show him the best night of his life. Description source: IMDB)

SOCIAL TRAITS

Getting Along with Others

WEEK 25:

Trust—Be Trustworthy and Trust Others Until They Prove Themselves Untrustworthy

Why can't you trust atoms?
Because they make up everything!

Extraordinary people have reputations of being trustworthy. If you aren't trustworthy, others will not want to do business with you or be your friend. Moreover, once a trust is broken, you will find it is practically impossible to regain that trust. You must be meticulous in both word and deed to earn a reputation for being trustworthy.

You should always be cautious in your business affairs, but in general, you should tend to trust people because most people are trustworthy most of the time. By being cautious, you should realize that if a deal seems to be too good to be true, it probably isn't true. Also, you should do your best to pay a fair price for services rendered. If you drive too hard for a bargain, it may come back to bite you in other ways, such as through shoddy work.

You must also be careful when describing others as untrustworthy with little basis for doing so. There is an old saying that often when people describe others, they are really describing themselves. What does that say about the person who says they think everyone is a cheat? Extraordinary people believe most people are trustworthy, at least until people demonstrate otherwise.

You should not be foolish about giving out your trust since it is good to be a bit cautious. Still, it is better to be too trusting and occasionally be disappointed than it is to always be on guard to the point of missing interesting experiences and knowing many wonderful people.

Be extraordinary by being trustworthy and trusting other people until they prove themselves to be untrustworthy.

"You may be deceived if you trust too much,
but you will live in torment if you don't trust enough."

Source: Frank Crane

Trust Film: *French Kiss*
Distributed by 20th Century Fox

(A woman flies to France to confront her straying fiancé, but gets
into trouble when the charming crook seated next to her uses her for
smuggling. Description source: IMDB)

WEEK 26:

Campaigning—Make Everyone Feel Important

A man in Texas tries to buy half a head of lettuce.

The young produce assistant tells him that they only sell whole heads of lettuce.

The man persists and asks to see the manager.

The boy says he'll ask his manager about it.

Walking into the back room, the boy said to his manager, "Some jerk wants to buy half a head of lettuce."

As he finished his sentence, he turned to find the man standing right behind him, so he added, "And this gentleman has offered to buy the other half."

The manager approved the deal, and the man went on his way.

Later the manager said to the boy, "I was impressed with the way you got yourself out of that situation earlier. We like people who think on their feet here. Where are you from, son?"

"Canada," replied the boy.

"Why did you leave Canada?" the manager asked.

The boy said, "Because there's nothing up there but whores and hockey players."

"Really?" said the manager. "My wife is from Canada."

"No kidding?" replied the boy. "What team did she play for?"

Wouldn't it be great if we could simply declare ourselves extraordinary? Unfortunately, we cannot. The position of "Extraordinary" is an elected position. The people who come into contact with us or have heard about us are the ones who will decide if we are extraordinary or not.

Ordinary people don't realize that they are campaigning every day and that everyone they meet is a voter. Ordinary people don't even know there is an election going on, which is why a limited number of opportunities come their way. Ordinary people don't appreciate the value in going out of their way to make others feel better about themselves. Ordinary people don't even bother to try to win over their coworkers. Little do they realize how much the opinions of coworkers can affect their own careers.

Extraordinary people, however, view every day as another day on the campaign trail, making friends of strangers, and winning over coworkers, the boss, and everyone else they meet. They pay particular attention to everyone, especially those of lower status who may need more of a boost to their self-esteem than others may. Their goal is to make sure everyone they meet feels respected and appreciated.

One of the best ways to have people think well of us is to make sure they think well of themselves. If we make them feel good about themselves, we can be sure that they will think well of us, or at least will consider us smart enough to recognize their talents. It never hurts to be generous with your compliments. Most people are starving for recognition of their efforts and validation of their self-worth.

Showing kindness to all without distinction creates a wonderful impression on those who observe you as well as on those to whom you extend your kindness. You don't have to do anything grand, though, and perhaps it is best you don't, as that could breed jealousy and envy. Small acts of kindness pay large dividends.

Another way to make people feel appreciated is to address them by name. Very few words sound as sweet to a person as their name. If you want to win people over, remember people's names and use those names frequently. Ordinary people tell themselves that they are not good at remembering names. Well, here is a secret: no one is! Since ordinary people know they are not good about remembering people's names, they don't try. There lies the difference between extraordinary people and ordinary people.

Be extraordinary by making everyone you interact with feel important.

"I've learned that people will forget what you said; people will forget what you did,
but people will never forget how you made them feel."

Source: Maya Angelou

Campaigning Film: *Bernie*
Distributed by Millennium Entertainment

(In small-town Texas, an affable mortician strikes up a friendship with
a wealthy widow, though when she starts to become controlling, he
goes to great lengths to separate himself from her grasp. Description
source: IMDB)

WEEK 27:

Friends—Be a Friend and You Will Have Friends

Friendship between Women:

A woman didn't come home one night.

The next day she told her husband she had slept over at a friend's house.

The man called his wife's ten best friends.

None of them knew about it.

Friendship between Men:

A man didn't come home one night.

The next day he told his wife he had slept over at a friend's house.

The woman called her husband's ten best friends.

Eight of them confirmed that he had slept over...

Two claimed that he was still there.

It is important to have true friends. You must treasure your true friends as they are rare and more valuable than any material object. A true friend is not jealous of your success; in fact, they try to encourage you to be successful. A true friend will risk your friendship to stop you from making a big mistake. The only way to have friends like this is to be that kind of friend to them.

Ordinary people may appear to have friends, but they tend to be fair weather friends who take pleasure when you are down. Oh, they may come to your assistance when you are down on your luck. In fact, they may like it that way. However, a true friend isn't someone who wants to help you when you are down; a true friend is someone who just wants to make sure you are always doing well.

There is an old saying that birds of a feather flock together. Like all sayings that have been around for a long time, there is truth to that statement. You need to surround yourself with extraordinary people; and if you want to change, you need to associate with people who represent that change.

You will find that some of your friends will gladly support your effort to change. However, you will also find that some of your old friends will become extremely jealous of the person you are becoming.

Be extraordinary by being a true friend and surrounding yourself with extraordinary friends.

"I value the friend who, for me, finds time on his calendar,
I cherish the friend who, for me, does not consult his calendar."
Source: Robert Brault

Friends Film: *Soul Men*
Distributed by Metro-Goldwyn-Mayer and Dimension Films

(Though it's been some twenty years since they have spoken with one another, two estranged soul-singing legends agree to participate in a reunion performance at the Apollo Theater to honor their recently deceased band leader. Description source: IMDB)

WEEK 28:

Diversity—Grow by Surrounding Yourself with People Different from Yourself

The following people found themselves stranded in the middle of nowhere:

Two Italian men and one Italian woman

Two French men and one French woman

Two German men and one German woman

Two Greek men and one Greek woman

Two English men and one English woman

Two Bulgarian men and one Bulgarian woman

Two Japanese men and one Japanese woman

Two Chinese men and one Chinese woman

One month later, on these deserted islands, the following things have occurred:

One Italian man killed the other Italian man for the Italian woman.

The two French men and the French woman are living happily together in a ménage à trois.

The two German men have a strict weekly schedule of alternating visits with the German woman.

The two Greek men are sleeping with each other and the Greek woman is cleaning and cooking for them.

The two English men are waiting for someone to introduce them to the English woman.

The two Bulgarian men took one look at the Bulgarian woman and started swimming to another island.

The two Japanese men have faxed Tokyo and are awaiting instructions.

The two Chinese men have set up a pharmacy/liquor store/laundry and restaurant and have gotten the woman pregnant in order to supply employees for their store.

Extraordinary people surround themselves with people much different from themselves as they recognize the opportunity to learn from others. We all see things differently based on our own experiences. So the more diverse our circle of friends and acquaintances, the broader our perspective is likely to become.

You need friends of different backgrounds, beliefs, genders, educations, professions, trades, cultures, races, sexual orientations, wealth levels, political beliefs, etc. Having such a variety of friends and acquaintances will enrich you and make you far from an ordinary person. Remember that every interaction with anyone always leaves a trace on you.

If you notice, ordinary people tend to associate with people just like themselves and are often intolerant of those different from themselves. Perhaps, some can only feel good about themselves if they look down upon someone else. Regardless of their reasons, by surrounding themselves with people just like they are, these ordinary people are missing many different perspectives, friendships, and adventures.

Be extraordinary, and grow by surrounding yourself with people different from yourself.

"The people you meet are all here to teach you something.

Your job is to try to determine what the people in your life are trying to teach you."

Source: Richard Carlson, PhD

Diversity Film: *Crash*
Distributed by Lionsgate (US) and Pathé (UK)

(Los Angeles citizens with vastly separate lives collide in interweaving stories of race, loss and redemption. Description source: IMDB)

WEEK 29:

Communicate—Listen to Others and Put Thought into Your Communications

A cat said, "Meow."

A second cat said, "Meow, Meow."

The first cat said, "Don't change the subject."

Ordinary people often fall into one of two groups of poor communicators.

The first group says little, if they communicate at all. They do not speak their minds, and if pushed, they give vague answers so as to offend no one. We rarely hear from them, and so they are rarely if ever in our thoughts.

The second group talks nonstop but says very little. They often sound like scripted soap operas. You usually know what they are going to say before they finish their sentence. They often use poor word choices, such as calling someone a liar over some small detail, when actually the individual was probably simply mistaken.

Ordinary people typically just listen to formulate their reply, rather than to understand what the other party is saying. Extraordinary people know that listening is one of the most powerful tools there is, both for learning and for winning over people.

Extraordinary people listen to understand and appreciate another's story, as well as to learn. They know you cannot learn much if you are the one doing the majority of the talking. Therefore, when communicating with another person, it is a good idea for you to consider which one of you is doing most of the listening.

Extraordinary people also pay close attention to what others do not say. Often, there is more meaning in what is not said than there is in what is actually said.

In addition to being good listeners, extraordinary people are also good communicators, both in writing and in speaking. They never stay out of contact too long.

Their communications are never manipulative. They use as few words as possible, which gives more weight to what they say. If you want to communicate concisely, you need to give some thought to what you plan to communicate. Usually you are better off limiting yourself to three points on any topic you are discussing. You should take care to choose correct and tactful words to express yourself, and sometimes it is best to say nothing at all.

Be extraordinary by listening to others and putting thought into what you communicate.

The tongue has the power of life and death.
"Who are you hurting today?
Who are you bringing back to life?"

Source: Stafford Whiteaker

Communicate Film: *A Thousand Words*
Distributed by Paramount Pictures and DreamWorks Pictures

(After stretching the truth on a deal with a spiritual guru, literary agent Jack McCall finds a Bodhi tree on his property. Its appearance holds a valuable lesson on the consequences of every word we speak. Description source: IMDB)

WEEK 30:

Arguments—Argue with No One

Jesus and Satan have an argument as to who is the better programmer. This goes on for a few hours until they come to an agreement to hold a contest, with God as the judge.

They type furiously, creating lines and lines of code. They keep at it for several hours straight. Seconds before the end of the competition, a bolt of lightning causes the electrical power to go out. The power comes back on and God announces that the contest is over.

He asks Satan to show what he has done. Satan is visibly upset, and cries, "I have nothing. I lost it all when the power went out."

"Very well, then," says God, "let us see if Jesus fared any better."

Jesus enters a command, and his screen comes to full life in a beautiful, vivid display. Just then, the voices of an angelic choir begin to pour forth from the speakers.

Satan is astonished. He stutters in disbelief, "B-b-but how? I lost everything, yet Jesus's program is intact! How did he do it?"

God chuckles, "Everybody knows…Jesus saves."

Extraordinary people have disagreements, whereas ordinary people have arguments. Ordinary people believe they can win any argument, which is why they engage in them. Just being in an argument automatically makes you ordinary. There is a saying that you can tell how big people are by what makes them angry. Do not let little things make you angry.

You must realize that it is not possible to win an argument. What tangible good comes to you from arguing? Even in the unlikely event that the other party admits you won, you have probably only won the other party's animosity toward you.

Since there is nothing to gain from arguments, do not engage in them. Why would you want to engage in any activity that causes animosity in another party, even a stranger, let alone a friend or even someone you are likely to see again? Many arguments are simply about opinions. You should remember that people have all sorts of opinions, and you should remember that they are entitled to their opinions, even if those opinions are mistaken. Not to mention, perhaps your own opinions may be mistaken.

When they do find themselves in an argument, extraordinary people do their best to find or create an exit so that all parties can maintain their pride.

Be extraordinary by arguing with no one.

"You get angry with someone and want to give that person a piece of your mind.

Wait.

Peace of mind just might show up."

Source: Victoria Moran

Argument Film: *The Big Lebowski*
Distributed by Gramercy Pictures

("Dude" Lebowski, mistaken for a millionaire Lebowski, seeks restitution for his ruined rug and enlists his bowling buddies to help get it. Description source: IMDB)

WEEK 31:

Gratitude—Express Gratitude at the Slightest Opportunity

A family was having dinner on Mother's Day. For some reason, the mother was unusually quiet.

Finally, the husband asked what was wrong.

"Nothing," said the woman.

Not buying it, he asked again. "Seriously, what's wrong?"

"Do you really want to know? Well, I'll tell you. I have cooked and cleaned and fed the kids for fifteen years, and on Mother's Day, you don't even tell me so much as 'thank you.'"

"Why should I?" he said. "Not once in fifteen years have I gotten a Father's Day gift."

"Yes," she said, "but I'm their real mother."

Extraordinary people express gratitude whenever possible, for even the slightest acts of kindness. Extraordinary people know that others like to feel appreciated for things they do. They know that if you make others feel good about their efforts, they will be more willing to assist again. No effort should go unacknowledged, regardless of how insignificant it may be, from letting you go through a door first, to refilling your cup of coffee at a restaurant without your asking.

Ordinary people aren't as diligent about expressing appreciation for small acts of kindness. They tell themselves "it is the person's job," or that the act is so minor there is little point in going out of the way to acknowledge it. This habit of failing to show appreciation shows up in how they react to gifts and pay raises. Ordinary people may think, "Since everyone gets a raise, what is the big deal about getting a raise?" The raise may have been less than they expected, so they certainly are not going to express appreciation. Worse still, they may think a thank-you is unnecessary if the raise was due to a contractual obligation.

Now, contrast this with the extraordinary person's show of gratitude by thanking their boss for the raise even if it was less than expected or it was contractually obligated. What do you think the impact is on the boss of having an employee thank him for a raise, even if the boss knows it was less than expected or contractual and everyone received the same amount?

Be extraordinary by expressing gratitude at the slightest opportunity.

The angel said, "You aren't happy. How can I help you?"

The poet replied, "I have everything. However, I lack only one thing. Can you give it to me?"

The angel happily said, "Sure. I can give you anything you desire."

The poet stared right into the angel's eyes. "I want happiness."

"All right," the angel nodded. And the angel proceeds to take away everything the poet possessed. The angel took away the poet's talent, destroyed his looks, robbed him of his riches, and killed his wife. The angel then left for heaven.

A month later, the angel appeared in front of the poet. The poet was lying on the ground, half-dead, hungry, and struggling for survival. The angel then returned him everything he once possessed and left for heaven again.

Two weeks later, the angel paid a visit to the poet. This time, the poet, together with his wife, thanked the angel profusely. He [had] finally found happiness.

Source: Unknown

Gratitude Film: *Thank You for Smoking*
Distributed by Fox Searchlight Pictures

(Satirical comedy follows the machinations of Big Tobacco's chief
spokesman, Nick Naylor, who spins on behalf of cigarettes while trying
to remain a role model for his twelve-year-old son.
Description source: IMDB)

WEEK 32:

Apologize—Without Being Asked, and Never Ask for an Apology

Teacher: What do you call a person who apologizes for making a mistake?

Boy: An honest man.

Teacher: Good. And what do you call a person who apologizes although he did not make a mistake?

Boy: A Boyfriend.

On the surface, it would seem that extraordinary people are too big to humble themselves by making a sincere apology. Actually, it is often ordinary people who are too small to offer a sincere apology, even when they know they have done wrong. If their wrong is so bad that they do feel compelled to offer an apology, they will always offer it with an excuse for their actions, which is no apology at all.

The extraordinary person is quick with an apology when they know they have wronged someone. There is a lot of truth in that old saying that says it takes a big person to apologize.

Another difference between extraordinary people and ordinary people is that ordinary people will often demand an apology if they feel wronged. It is a power game with them. They want to see if they can force an apology from someone, especially if that person is of a higher social status. Extraordinary people know that a forced apology is no apology at all.

Be extraordinary by apologizing without offering an excuse, and never ask for an apology.

"Never ruin an apology with an excuse."

Source: Benjamin Franklin

Apologize Film: *Trouble with the Curve*
Distributed by Warner Bros.

(An ailing baseball scout in his twilight years takes his daughter along for one last recruiting trip. Description source: IMDB)

WEEK 33:

"No"—Always say "No" at the Slightest Doubt

Father Murphy goes into a local bar in Dublin and approaches the first man he sees and says, "Do you want to go to Heaven?" The man replied, "Indeed I do, Father." Father Murphy commands, "Then for God's sake, leave this pub right now."

Father Murphy then goes to the next man, "Do you want to go to Heaven, my son?" And the man answers, "Yes Father, indeed I want to do that very thing." Father Murphy orders, "Then ye must get out of this pub right now!"

Father Murphy continues this throughout the pub until he comes to the last man. "Do you want to go to Heaven, man?" The man looks at his half-full beer, turns, looks at Father Murphy and says, "No, I don't, Father." A shocked Father Murphy replies, "You mean to tell me, young man, that when you die, you don't want to go to Heaven?" The young man replies, "Oh, well, when I die, yes, Father, I certainly do. I thought you were getting a group together to go right now!"

"No" is a powerful aid in your campaign to be extraordinary. "No" can save you a lot of time, money, and bad feelings, both your own and those that others may have about you if you fail to meet their expectations. Any bad feelings toward you generated from your "no" will be far less bad than those that arise from failing to do something you agreed to do without really thinking about it.

"No" is quick, and so the pain is short-lived for both you and whomever you are responding to. In addition, on later reflection, you can change your mind if that is what you really want to do. Also, your later "yes" may result in more positive feelings toward you than if you immediately said "yes," since people don't really appreciate things that come too easily.

Surely, you have noticed that many ordinary people simply cannot say "no" to anything. They simply don't own enough of themselves. At best, they may not answer, which is a coward's way of saying "no." Therefore, when a person says "no" to you, the extraordinary thing to do is simply to thank them. If you push them, you may get them to say "yes." However, they may not come through since they didn't want to say "yes" in the first place. The failure of them to come through for you may make bigger problems for you than had the answer initially been "no."

From your own standpoint, there is nothing wrong with saying "no," since it clears the way to say "yes" to something more important to you. Think back to any time you have wanted to do something and said to yourself that you simply didn't have time to do it. This is an indication that you are saying "yes" to activities that are of lower value to you than the activity you wanted to do. If you want time for important things, make time by frequently and decisively saying "no" to less important activities.

An extraordinary person always says "no" at the slightest doubt.

"No" is a complete sentence and so often we forget that.

When we don't want to do something we can simply smile and say "No."

We don't have to explain ourselves; we can just say "No."

Early in my journey, I found developing the ability to say "no" expanded my ability to say "yes" and really mean it.

"Love yourself enough to be able to say 'yes' or 'no.'"

Source: Susan Gregg

"No" Film: *No Reservations*
Distributed by Warner Bros.

(The life of a top chef changes when she becomes the guardian of her young niece. Description source: IMDB)

WEEK 34:

Generosity—A Scrooge Can Never Be Extraordinary

One evening a Scotsman was riding in his limousine when he saw two men along the road eating grass.

Disturbed, he yelled at his driver to stop and got out to investigate.

He asked one man, "Why are you eating the grass?"

"Well, we don't have any money for food," the poor man replied. "So we have to eat grass."

"Well then, come with me to my house and I'll feed you," the Scotsman said.

"But sir, I also have a wife and two children with me. They are over there, under that tree."

"OK, bring them along, too," the Scotsman replied.

Turning to the other poor man he stated, "You come with us, also."

The second man, in a pitiful voice, then said, "But sir, I also have a wife and seven children with me!"

"Very well then, bring them all," the Scotsman answered.

They all piled into the limousine, which was no easy task.

Once under way, one of the poor fellows turned to the Scotsman and said, "Sir, you are truly too kind. Thank you for taking all of us with you."

The Scotsman replied, "No problem, glad to do it. You'll really love my place. The grass is almost a foot high."

No doubt, someone is asking you daily, via telephone, mail, e-mail, or in person, to give to this or that cause. You should act on your generous impulses. However, know that many solicitors are paid and they are asking you to donate to charitable organizations whose executives often make six or seven figure incomes. Charity has become a business. Before donating, you should know how much of your donation actually goes to the intended recipients. It can be as low as fifteen cents of every dollar you give. If possible, you may want to eliminate the intermediaries and give directly to a person or organization you want to support.

As helpful as financial generosity can be, the best form of generosity is giving your time, your concern, your knowledge, and your love to another person. But, time is your most precious gift because it is irreplaceable, so be extremely careful with your gifts of time. You must remember that there is a reason the airlines tell you to put the oxygen masks on yourself first. You cannot help anyone unless you first help yourself. So use your time to maintain your health, develop yourself, and maintain your relationships; then you can donate the remainder of your time to helping others. Too many ordinary people spend so much of their time helping others that they neglect themselves and before long cannot even help themselves, let alone others.

You will never be extraordinary with the reputation of being a cheapskate. There is nothing more ordinary than the person who rarely, if ever, picks up the tab. However, you do not want to be at the opposite extreme of always picking up the tab, since it can easily result in envy and resentment. Also, you need to be aware of those who think you should always pay because you have more money than they do. Often, they aren't even grateful for you paying because they consider you to be rich and so it is no big deal for you always to pay. They never factor in the sacrifices you made to acquire the money you have, while they may have saved nothing and quit jobs they didn't like before finding others. And of course, it is always best to give to those who need, but don't ask or expect.

One often hears that what we give comes back to us and usually with interest. I believe that is true, but I also realize that those always in need seem to be especially fond of this saying.

Remember, a scrooge can never be extraordinary; be generous to those who are deserving of your generosity.

"No person was ever honored for what he received.

Honor has been the reward for what he gave."

Source: Calvin Coolidge

Generosity Film: *Scrooged*
Distributed by Paramount Pictures

(A selfish, cynical T.V. executive is haunted by three spirits bearing lessons on Christmas Eve. Description source: IMDB)

WEEK 35:

Gossip—Don't

Four clergymen, taking a short break from their heavy schedules, were sitting on a park bench, chatting and enjoying an early spring day.

"You know, since all of us are such good friends," said one, "this might be a good time to discuss personal problems." They all agreed.

"Well, I would like to share with you the fact that I drink to excess," said one. There was a gasp from the other three.

Then another spoke up. "Since you were so honest, I'd like to say that my big problem is gambling. It's terrible, I know, but I can't quit. I've even been tempted to take money from the collection plate."

Another gasp was heard, and then the third clergyman spoke, "I'm really troubled, brothers, because I'm growing fond of a woman in my church—a married woman." More gasps.

But the fourth clergyman remained silent. After a few minutes, the others coaxed him to open up.

"The fact is," he said, "I just don't know how to tell you about my problem."

"It's all right, brother. Your secret is safe with us," said the others.

"Well, it's this way," he said. "You see, I'm an incurable gossip."

How rare it is to find someone who doesn't engage in gossip. It is about as rare as finding an extraordinary person because extraordinary people don't engage in gossip. They discuss more interesting things than the problems of other people. When the extraordinary person does happen to hear about another person's difficulties, rather than engaging in gossiping about that person's plight, the extraordinary person tries to help that person.

Ordinary people seem to delight in discussing the problems of others, perhaps because it makes them feel better about themselves. It's hard to find much good that comes from such conversations. Gossiping is even worse when the information is inaccurate.

Be extraordinary, and don't gossip.

"Our worst fault is our preoccupation with the faults of others."

Source: Kahlil Gibran

Gossip Film: *Did You Hear About the Morgans?*
Distributed by Columbia Pictures

(In New York City, an estranged couple who witness a murder are relocated to small-town Wyoming as part of a witness-protection program. Description source: IMDB)

WEEK 36:

Smile—You Will Feel Better and So Will Everyone Who Comes in Contact with You

Three dead bodies turn up at the mortuary,
all with very big smiles on their faces. The coroner calls the police
inspector to ask what has happened.

"First body: Frenchman, sixty, died of heart failure while making love
to his mistress. Hence the enormous smile, Inspector," says the coroner.

"Second body: Scotsman, twenty-five, won a thousand dollars on the
lottery, spent it all on whisky. Died of alcohol poisoning, hence the
smile."

The inspector asked, "What of the third body?"

"Ah," says the coroner, "this is the most unusual one.
Billy-Bob, the redneck from Oklahoma, thirty, struck by lightning."

"Why is he smiling then?" inquires the inspector.

"Thought he was having his picture taken."

Smiling is such a simple act; it actually makes you feel better as well as everyone who encounters you. Smiles are contagious, and people like to be around those who make them feel good.

Frowns and general grumpiness are also contagious. Chances are that if you go around with a frown on your face and a grumpy attitude, you will meet many people with frowns on their faces and grumpy attitudes. Many ordinary people create such a world for themselves, since in one way or another we all create our own reality.

Be extraordinary. Smile, and create your own positive environment.

"A smile shortens the distance between two people."

Source: Unknown

Smile Film: *The Artist*
Distributed by Warner Bros. (France),
The Weinstein Company (US/AUS) and Entertainment Film
Distributors (UK)

(A silent movie star meets a young dancer, but the arrival of talking
pictures sends their careers in opposite directions."
Description source: IMDB)

LEARNING TRAITS

Growth Keeps You Extraordinary

WEEK 37:

Time—Use Your Time Wisely

"No man goes before his time,

unless the boss leaves early."

Extraordinary people use their time wisely. Every person on earth gets the same twenty-four hours. Ordinary people may claim they don't have time for this or that, but the truth is that they have as much time as anyone. If they were more honest with themselves, they would admit the activity in question is of lower value to them than what they are currently doing or what they plan to do with that time. What you choose to do with your time is what will make you extraordinary.

How many times have you agreed to something that you know wasn't the best use of your time? How many times have you continued watching a television show or movie that wasn't entertaining or informative? If you think about it, you will likely conclude that consuming more entertainment is vastly overrated.

Books are especially hard to stop once you start them. You think, "I have so much time invested in the book already, how can I stop?" However, that time already invested in the book is gone. You can't get that time back. What is important is what you do with the next moment, hour, or day of your life and perhaps you would rather do something else with your time.

Extraordinary people, like everyone else, will get older. Nevertheless, they do not let their age stop them from starting projects, even ones that take years to complete. After all, they are going to continue aging, whether or not they start the project. People have accomplished many great things in their later years.

You constantly need to seek to eliminate your low value activities in favor of activities you find more meaningful, such as spending more time on your relationships, learning, or doing whatever is important to you. The key word is "important," and not simply doing more, faster.

Be extraordinary, and use your precious time wisely.

Washington, DC, Metro Station on a cold January morning in 2007. A man with a violin played six Bach pieces for about forty-five minutes. During that time, about two thousand people went through the station, most of them on their way to work.
After three minutes, a middle-aged man noticed the musician playing. He slowed his pace and stopped for a few seconds, then hurried to meet his schedule.

4 minutes later:

The violinist received his first dollar: a woman threw the money in the hat and, without stopping, continued walking.

6 minutes:

A young man leaned against the wall to listen to him, then looked at his watch and started to walk again.

10 minutes:

A three-year-old boy stopped but his mother tugged him along hurriedly. The kid stopped to look at the violinist again, but the mother pushed hard and the child continued walking, turning his head all the time. Several other children repeated these actions. Every parent, without exception, forced his or her children to move on quickly.

45 minutes:

The musician had played continuously. Only six people had stopped and listened for a short while. About twenty gave money but continued walking at their normal pace. The man collected a total of thirty-two dollars.

1 hour:

He finished playing and silence took over. No one noticed, no one applauded, nor was there any recognition. No one knew this, but the violinist was Joshua Bell, one of the greatest musicians in the world. He played one of the most intricate pieces ever written, with a violin worth three and a half million dollars. Two days before, Joshua Bell sold out a theater in Boston where the seats averaged a hundred dollars apiece.

The questions raised:

In a common environment at an inappropriate hour, do we perceive beauty?

Do we stop to appreciate it?

Do we recognize talent in an unexpected context?

One possible conclusion reached from this experiment could be this:

If we don't have a moment to stop and listen to one of the best musicians in the world, playing some of the finest music ever written, with one of the most beautiful instruments ever made...
How many other things are we missing?

Time Film: *Somewhere in Time*
Distributed by Universal Pictures

(A Chicago playwright uses self-hypnosis to find the actress whose vintage portrait hangs in a grand hotel. Description source: IMDB)

WEEK 38:

*80/20 Rule—80 Percent of Your Outcomes Come from
20 Percent of Your Inputs*

There was a perfect man and a perfect woman. They met each other at a perfect party. They dated for two perfect years. They had the perfect wedding and the perfect honeymoon.

One day the perfect man and the perfect woman were driving in their perfect car and saw an elf by the side of the road. Being perfect people, they picked him up.

As the perfect man and perfect woman were driving with the elf, they got into an accident. Two people died and one lived.

Who died and who lived?

The perfect woman lived because the perfect man and elves aren't real.

Extraordinary people are efficient; they live by the 80/20 rule, or Pareto principle, which says that 80 percent of our results come from 20 percent of our inputs or efforts.

Instead of trying to be a perfectionist like many ordinary people, you should aim high, but not for perfection. The extraordinary people use the time saved to enjoy their lives and the people around them. The strain that goes toward perfection is rarely worth the effort, let alone the cost to one's relationships.

Many ordinary people wrongly focus on their exertion rather than their production. They look busy, work extra hours and skip lunches to appear heroic. However, their additional efforts add little extra value to the outcomes. Extraordinary people prefer to impress with results.

The 80/20 rule applies to everything, even your clothing. If you pay attention, you'll probably notice that you wear 20 percent of your clothing 80 percent of the time. As for friends, you probably spend 80 percent of your time socializing with 20 percent of your acquaintances.

Be extraordinary, and apply the 80/20 rule to all aspects of your life.

"Nothing is less productive than to make more efficient what should not be done at all."

Source: Peter Drucker

80/20 Rule Film: *Win Win*
Distributed by Fox Searchlight Pictures

(A struggling lawyer and volunteer wrestling coach's chicanery comes back to haunt him when the teenage grandson of the client he's double-crossed comes into his life. Description source: IMDB)

WEEK 39:

Delegate—You Can't Do Everything Yourself

A man who had started a small business was interviewing a young man for an accounting position.

"I need someone with an accounting degree," the man said. "But mainly, I'm looking for someone to do my worrying for me."

"Excuse me?" the accountant said.

The man said, "I don't want to have to worry about money. Your job will be to take all the money worries off my back."

"I see," the accountant said. "And how much does the job pay?"

"I'll start you at eighty thousand."

"Eighty thousand dollars!" the accountant exclaimed. "How can such a small business afford a sum like that?"

"That," the owner said, "is your first worry."

Extraordinary people know they don't have enough time or skills to do everything that they need to do. However, there are many activities that people can do, but that they may not wish to do because they prefer to use their time in other ways.

For instance, heads of dental practices can choose to perform all the root canal procedures while leaving the fillings and crowns to the dentists that work in their practices. These head dentists could do the fillings and crowns, but they find it more advantageous to delegate these tasks.

In turn, those dentists could clean teeth, but they delegate these procedures to skilled dental hygienists so they can focus on fillings, crowns, etc.

The dental hygienists could clean their own houses and mow their own lawns, but prefer to work extra hours with the time they save by hiring out these activities.

Many ordinary people want to do everything themselves, telling themselves delegation takes longer than simply doing the task themselves. When they do delegate, they save very little time because they are so busy overseeing what they delegated. In addition, whoever they delegated the task to will likely become frustrated with all the oversight and end up doing the work poorly.

When extraordinary people delegate, they do so without micromanaging the task; instead, they simply tell someone else the task and the purpose of the task. Telling the person the purpose of the task is often important. For instance, you may say you want a table cleaned. If you want the table cleaned so that you can write on the table, that calls for one way of cleaning the table. If you want to serve dinner on the table, it calls for another type of cleaning. In the unlikely event you want to perform an operation on the table, that calls for still another type of cleaning.

Be extraordinary by delegating properly and without micromanaging the delegated task.

"Don't tell people how to do things.
Tell them what to do and let them surprise you with the results."

Source: George S. Patton

Delegate Film: *Get Him to the Greek*
Distributed by Universal Pictures

(A record company intern is hired to accompany out-of-control British
rock star Aldous Snow to a concert at L.A.'s Greek Theater. Description
source: IMDB)

WEEK 40:

Seeing and Hearing—See and Hear What Is There, Rather than What You Want to Be There

A man goes to a bar with his dog. He goes up to the bar and asks for a drink. The bartender says, "You can't bring that dog in here!"

The guy, without missing a beat, says, "This is my guide dog."

"Oh man," the bartender says, "I'm sorry. Here, the first one's on me." The man takes his drink and goes to a table near the door.

Another guy walks in the bar with a Chihuahua. The first guys sees him, stops him, and says, "You can't bring that dog in here unless you tell him it's a guide dog."

The second man graciously thanks the first man and continues to the bar. He asks for a drink.

The bartender says, "Hey, you can't bring that dog in here!"

The second man replies, "This is my guide dog."

The bartender says, "No, I don't think so. They do not have Chihuahuas as guide dogs."

The man pauses for a half second and replies, "What? They gave me a Chihuahua?"

Ordinary people see and hear what they want to see and hear. They simply will not recognize things that are contrary to their beliefs and instead make excuses for what they saw or heard.

The extraordinary person knows that people show you who they really are in so many little ways, such as how they treat restaurant servers, receptionists, and sales clerks. They tell you about themselves by how they describe others. They also tell you about themselves through their generosity or lack of generosity. Moreover, sometimes people simply tell you something directly about themselves that contradicts your view of them. Ordinary people will ignore this information if it contradicts their image of a person.

And, as much as possible, the extraordinary person tries to see what isn't there. An example would be a missing wedding ring on someone who you know is married. Sometimes the absence of things tells you more than what is present. In addition, you need to look deeply at what you do see. An example of looking deeply is seeing an iceberg; it may not seem so large, but you know that the portion of the iceberg below the water is far larger than what you actually see above the water. And of course, you always need to be open to seeing the unexpected; otherwise, you may miss something important.

Be extraordinary, and pay attention to what you see and hear as well as what you don't see and hear.

"Each of us tends to think we see things
as they are, that we are objective.

But this is not the case.
We see the world not as it is, but as we are conditioned to see it.

When we open our mouths to describe what we see, we in effect
describe ourselves, our perceptions, our paradigms."

Source: Stephen Covey

Seeing and Hearing Film: *Michael*
Distributed by New Line Cinema

(Two tabloid reporters checking out a report of the Archangel Michael living with an old woman find that it's true. But that's not the only surprise. Description source: IMDB)

WEEK 41:

Journaling—Formally Analyze Your Day in a Journal

In Jerusalem, a female journalist heard about a very old Jewish man who had been going to the Wailing Wall to pray twice a day, every day, for a long, long time. So she went to the Wailing Wall, and there he was!

She watched him pray, and after about forty-five minutes, when he turned to leave, she approached him for an interview. "Sir, how long have you been coming to the Wall and praying?"

"For about sixty years."

"Sixty years! That's amazing! What do you pray for?"

"I pray for peace between the Christians, Jews, and the Muslims. I pray for all the hatred to stop, and I pray for all our children to grow up in safety and friendship."

"How do you feel after doing this for sixty years?"

"I feel like I'm talking to a wall."

Ordinary people rarely reflect at all, let alone reflect on each day to the point of putting their thoughts in a journal.

If you wish to be extraordinary, it will help to develop the habit of formally analyzing your day in a journal, noting what made you feel extraordinary and what made you feel ordinary that day.

You can select any form of journaling, from writing in a journal to typing each day's activity in a computerized log. Record what you wish, but be sure to record anything that day that made you feel extraordinary and anything that made you feel ordinary. You can use this information to make your next day better. After a year, you can start your day by not only looking at the prior day but also what you did a year ago that made you feel extraordinary and ordinary. You can use the insights from this analysis to make progress toward being the extraordinary person you want to be. You will have disappointing days, but over the year, you will become more extraordinary.

Be extraordinary by developing the habit of formally analyzing your day in a journal.

"The discipline of writing something down is the first step toward making it happen."

Source: Lee Iacocca

Journaling Film: *Burn After Reading*
Distributed by Focus Features

(A disk containing the memoirs of a CIA agent ends up in the hands of two unscrupulous gym employees who attempt to sell it.
Description source: IMDB)

WEEK 42:

Goals—Set Goals, Make Plans to Achieve Them, and
Monitor Your Progress

Dan was a single guy living at home with his father and working in the
family business.
When he found out he was going to inherit a fortune when his sickly
father died, he decided he needed a wife to share his fortune.
One evening at an investment meeting, he spotted the most beautiful
woman he had ever seen.
"I may look like just an ordinary man," he said to her, "but in just a few
years, my father will die, and I'll inherit two hundred million dollars."
Impressed, the woman obtained his business card and three days later,
she became his stepmother.

Extraordinary people set goals and develop specific action plans to achieve them, whereas ordinary people don't see the point in all that planning.

Extraordinary people put their plans in writing because writing forces them to be precise. They make their goals specific as to quantity, quality, and time.

Extraordinary people put a lot of effort into developing action plans. They set interim target dates so that they know if they are making progress or need to take corrective action.

Extraordinary people share their plans with others as a way of holding themselves accountable. Their goals are objectively verifiable, so others know how they are progressing. Ordinary people, even if they develop goals, avoid this level of accountability.

When it comes to setting goals, extraordinary people know they need goals that stretch them, but not so challenging that they are impossible to achieve.

Extraordinary people know that it is a mistake to set too many goals. They believe with time and effort, they can accomplish almost all, but perhaps not everything, they want to do.

Be extraordinary by setting specific goals, making plans to achieve those goals, and finding someone to monitor your progress.

"The greatest danger for most of us is not that our aim is too
high and we miss it,
but that it is too low and we reach it."

Source: Michelangelo

Goals Film: *The Bucket List*
Distributed by Warner Bros. Pictures

(Two terminally ill men escape from a cancer ward and head off on a
road trip with a wish list of to-dos before they die.
Description source: IMDB)

WEEK 43:

Prioritize—You Can Do Anything You Want to Do,
Just Not Everything You Want to Do

A group of friends went deer hunting and paired off for the day. That night, one of the hunters returned alone, staggering under an eight-point buck.

His friends asked, "Where's Harry?"

"Harry had a stroke of some kind. He's a couple of miles back up the trail."

"You left Harry lying there and carried the deer back?"

"Well," said the hunter, "I figured no one was going to steal Harry."

Ordinary people tend to put off important tasks by taking care of minor things. They tell themselves that once they do this or that, they will start on the more important task. However, they never seem to get around to that important task because it is so large or so unpleasant.

You, unlike ordinary people, know that the best way to tackle a big task is to break it up into smaller tasks that you can take on each day until you have completed the entire project. As for those truly unpleasant tasks, you know it is better to simply handle them rather than have them hanging over your head.

Be extraordinary by remembering you can do almost anything you want to do, but you just can't do everything you want to do.

A professor of philosophy stood before his class with some items in front of him. When the class began, wordlessly he picked up a large empty mayonnaise jar and proceeded to fill it with rocks about two inches in diameter. He then asked the students if the jar was full.

They agreed that it was full.

So the professor then picked up a box of pebbles and poured them into the jar. He shook the jar lightly and watched as the pebbles rolled into the open areas between the rocks. The professor then asked the students again if the jar was full.

They chuckled and agreed that it was indeed full this time.

The professor picked up a box of sand and poured it into the jar. The sand filled the remaining open areas of the jar. "Now," said the professor, "I want you to recognize that this jar signifies your life. The rocks are the truly important things, such as family, health and relationships. If all else was lost and only the rocks remained, your life would still be meaningful. The pebbles are the other things that matter in your life, such as work or school. The sand signifies the remaining "small stuff" and material possessions.

If you put sand into the jar first, there is no room for the rocks or the pebbles. The same applies to your life. If you spend all your time and energy on the small stuff, you will never have room for the things that are truly important.

Source: Unknown

Prioritize Film: *Bedazzled*
Distributed by 20th Century Fox

(Hopeless dweeb Elliot Richards is granted seven wishes by the devil
to snare Allison, the girl of his dreams, in exchange for his soul.
Description source: IMDB)

WEEK 44:

Expertise—Take Time to Study and Improve Your Skills

After unclogging the sink, a plumber hands the homeowner his bill.

"My gosh," said the homeowner, "I'm an attorney,
and I don't make that much an hour."

The plumber replied, "Neither did I when I was an attorney."

Extraordinary people are constantly updating their skills and their tools. That is because they realize that success in life calls for continuous improvement.

Ordinary people tend to think that if it isn't broke, don't fix it. If their current skill level and tools are generating the degree of success they are comfortable with, why should they change? Well, they should change because things do not stand still. Although their skills and tools may work for them today, that may not be true tomorrow.

Also, people are often so busy working that they feel they don't have the time to invest in additional training. Please don't make that mistake. You must set aside time to improve your skills or research tools that will make you even more successful, regardless of your current level of success.

You must continuously improve, if you want to be extraordinary.

"To face tomorrow with the thought of using the methods of yesterday is to envision life at a standstill."

Source: James F. Bell

Expertise Film: *Groundhog Day*
Distributed by Columbia Pictures

(A weatherman finds himself living the same day over and over again. Description source: IMDB)

WEEK 45:

Work—Choose Work You Love, Treat Your Coworkers Like Family and Friends, but Remember You Are Not Your Job

A mother came into her son's bedroom to wake him up. She said, "Time to get up and get ready for school."

Her son pulled the covers up over his face and said, "I'm not going to school this morning."

His mother asked, "Why aren't you going to school? Are you sick?"

"No, I'm not sick," her son replied, "but I'm not going to school."

"If you're not sick, why aren't you going to school?"

"I'm not going to school because I don't like it there. The kids hate me, and the teachers hate me, and I'm not going anymore."

Pulling the covers off him, his mother said, "It doesn't matter if the kids hate you and the teachers hate you. You're forty years old, and you're the principal. Get up. You're going to school."

Source: Rabbi Wayne Dosick

Work is one area where extraordinary people and ordinary people separate themselves in so many ways.

Ordinary people often just take whatever work comes their way. If they decide on a line of work, they often choose a job because they believe it will pay them more than other jobs. They may even take jobs that they realize are harmful to others because the jobs pay them well. They give little thought to whether the job is interesting, meaningful, or work that they can feel proud about.

Extraordinary people look for work that is humane, that they like, and that contributes to the public good. Studies indicate that those going into jobs they like do better financially than those going into a line of work for the money. Even if you could earn more doing something else, wouldn't you rather spend the larger part of your life doing something you love and that gives you a feeling of pride?

When ordinary people become dissatisfied with their jobs, some simply quit without first finding another job, whereas extraordinary people stick it out no matter how bad until they can find another position.

In addition, extraordinary people are willing to do lowly jobs as best they can, probably better than anyone else has done that job before. They don't look at any type of work as something beneath them. They simply perform to the best of their abilities while looking for something more challenging. With this attitude, they rarely stay in lowly jobs for long.

Many ordinary people believe their lives don't begin until they leave work. Therefore, they miss opportunities to build lasting relationships with their coworkers. Extraordinary people see their coworkers as friends and family and treat them as such.

However, extraordinary people must guard against thinking they are their jobs. The danger of identifying too closely with your work is that the unplanned loss of a job can be devastating to your self-esteem.

Be extraordinary by choosing work you love, treating your coworkers like family and friends, and remembering you are not your job.

Back in the Middle Ages, a dispatcher went to a building site in France.

He approached the first worker and asked, "What are you doing?"

"What are you, blind?" the worker snapped back. "I'm cutting these impossible boulders with primitive tools and putting them together the way the boss tells me. I'm sweating under this blazing sun; it's backbreaking work, and it's boring me to death!"

The dispatcher quickly backed off and retreated to a second worker. He asked the same question. "What are you doing?"

The worker replied, "I'm shaping these boulders into useable forms, which are then assembled according to the architect's plans. It's hard work and sometimes it gets repetitive, but I earn five francs a week, and that supports the wife and kids. It's a job. Could be worse."

Somewhat encouraged, the dispatcher went on to a third worker. "And what are you doing?" he asked.

"Why, can't you see?" said the worker as he lifted his arm to the sky, "I'm building a cathedral!"

Source: Edward Pulling

Work Film: *The Devil Wears Prada*
Distributed by 20th Century Fox

(A naive young woman comes to New York and scores a job as the assistant to one of the city's biggest magazine editors, the ruthless and cynical Miranda Priestly. Description source: IMDB)

WEEK 46:

Reading—Your Opportunity to Learn from Others

The army drafted me and so I wanted to fail my physical.

During my physical, the doctor asked softly, "Can you read the letters on the wall?"

"What letters?" I answered slyly.

"Good," said the doctor. "You passed the hearing test."

The person who doesn't read is no better off than the person who can't read. So when someone asks you if you read, please don't answer: "You mean books?"

Reading is your opportunity to hear what the great people of the past have to say to you. Reading is a way to gather fresh perspectives and to learn about things that you may never experience firsthand.

Ordinary people don't read, or if they do read, it certainly isn't worthwhile literature. They don't carry reading material around with them, so you often see them just waiting, doing nothing.

Extraordinary people are also subject to having to wait due to various situations; however, they use their time productively by reading worthwhile materials.

Speaking of reading worthwhile materials, as you are reading something, you may discover that it isn't as worthwhile as you initially thought it was. Well, no matter how much time you have invested in reading something—stop reading. There is no need for you to waste additional time. Many ordinary people cannot bring themselves to do this, so they end up wasting even more time reading something that offers no benefit to them.

The extraordinary person knows that to receive the most benefit from reading, they should read a wide variety of materials.

Be extraordinary by reading worthwhile materials.

"What you are today and what you will be in five years depends on two things:

The people you meet and the books you read."

Source: Twyla Tharp

Reading Film: *Fahrenheit 451*
Distributed by Universal Pictures

(In an oppressive future, a fireman whose duty is to destroy all books begins to question his task. Description source: IMDB)

WEEK 47:

Strategy—If It Is Worth Doing, It Is Worth Developing a Strategy

A businessperson was talking with his barber when they both noticed a goofy-looking fellow bouncing down the sidewalk. The barber whispered, "That's Tommy, one of the stupidest kids you'll ever meet. Here, I'll show you."
"Hey Tommy! Come here!" yelled the barber.
Tommy came bouncing over. "Hi Mr. Williams!"
The barber pulled out a rusty dime and a shiny quarter and told Tommy he could keep the one of his choice.
Tommy looked long and hard at the dime and quarter and then quickly snapped the dime from the barber's hand.
The barber looked at the businessperson and said, "See, I told you."
After his haircut, the businessperson caught up with Tommy and asked him why he chose the dime.
Tommy looked him in the eye and said, "If I take the quarter, the game is over."

Ordinary people go into situations, as well as life, without a plan. They simply let things happen to them, while hoping for the best; that is, if they think at all about what they are going into. If you don't develop a strategy for how you want something to turn out, there is a good chance it will not turn out to your benefit.

The extraordinary person always develops a strategy for anything of significance, be it a phone call, a meeting, or a purchase. If something is worth doing, it is worth developing some kind of strategy to make it turn out well for you.

When you speak, keep in mind not only the impact on your listeners, but also on those that may hear what you said second hand. You should consider the impact of even minor actions. In addition, when it comes to large-scale speeches and actions, you can't go wrong rehearsing and planning in detail what you will say and do. Doing so will give you confidence.

Your strategy should account for the likelihood that you will encounter obstacles or even resistance to your plans from others.

However, even the best strategies are useless if your motives aren't noble. Any arrangement you make should benefit the other party as much as it benefits you. It has to be a win-win for everyone. In the end, it is harmful to your success if people know your motives are purely self-interest and that you will take advantage of others.

Be extraordinary; if something is worth doing, it is worth developing a strategy to make it turn out well for you and the other party.

"Failing to prepare is preparing to fail."

Source: John Wooden

Strategy Film: *The Giant Mechanical Man*
Distributed by Tribeca Films

(An offbeat romantic comedy about a silver-painted street performer
and the soft spoken zoo worker who falls for him.
Description source: IMDB)

WEEK 48:

Travel—See Your Country as Well as the Rest of the World

An American man, a Russian man, and an African man were all up in a hot air balloon together. After a few minutes, the Russian man put his hand down through the clouds. "Aah!" he said. "We're right over my homeland."
"How can you tell?" asked the American.
"I can feel the cold air," he replied.
A few hours later, the African man put his hand through the clouds. "Aah! We're right over my homeland," he said.
"How do you know that?" asked the Russian.
"I can feel the warm air."
Several more hours later, the American put his hand through the clouds. "Aah! We're right over New York."
The Russian and the African were amazed. "How do you know all of that?" they exclaimed.

The American pulled his hand up. "My watch is missing."

Extraordinary people travel around their own countries and, every so often, outside of them.

Ordinary people may tell themselves that they cannot afford to travel. However, such statements probably say more about their priorities than they do about their financial conditions. The ordinary person tends to purchase objects, whereas the extraordinary person tends to purchase experiences.

As often as possible, our travels should take us some place that we haven't been before. Doing so will give us a broader perspective and bring excitement to our lives, as well as make us more interesting people. When someone mentions a place, we can comment from having actually been there.

Extraordinary people always pack a "good attitude" for any trip. They will not let being taken advantage of spoil their trip. Nor will they let the usual inconveniences bother them, whereas ordinary people may let such things spoil their trip.

Be extraordinary, and see your own country as well as the rest of the world.

"Travel is fatal to prejudice, bigotry, and narrow-mindedness."

Source: Mark Twain

Travel Film: *The Darjeeling Limited*
Distributed by Fox Searchlight Pictures

(A year after their father's funeral, three brothers travel across India by train in an attempt to bond with each other.
Description source: IMDB)

MISCELLANEOUS

The Odds and Ends of Being Extraordinary

WEEK 49:

Addictions—Don't Be Addicted to Anything

A mechanic noticed his coworker drinking brake fluid at lunch.

"What are you doing, man? You can't drink that stuff!"

"Relax," replied his coworker, "this stuff tastes pretty good, and I don't drink it all the time."

"Seriously," the mechanic exclaimed, "that brake fluid is poison!"

"Hey, man" yelled the coworker, "back off! I can stop any time I want."

You can never be extraordinary if you are addicted to anything. You cannot rid yourself of an addiction until you acknowledge your addiction and the power it has over you.

We typically think of addiction in terms of drugs and alcohol because that is often the case. But think of all the powerful people you have heard of who have been brought down by sex scandals. These people were addicted to sex. Then we have those who are slowly killing themselves by their addictions to nicotine, sugar, or white flour. Others become addicted to money, power, fame, and other things.

If you permit yourself to be controlled by something outside of yourself, you cannot be extraordinary or stay extraordinary. Extraordinary people develop a sense of detachment. If you can let things go, all control will rest within yourself.

Be extraordinary by not being addicted to anything.

"Shame was an emotion he had abandoned years earlier.

Addicts know no shame.

You disgrace yourself so many times you become immune to it."

John Grisham, *The Testament*

Addiction Film: *I Want Someone to Eat Cheese With*
Distributed by IFC Films

(About a man who has trouble with his job, trouble with women, and uses food to deal with it all. Description source: IMDB)

WEEK 50:

Marriage/Life Partners—Choose a Significant Other Who You Can Support and Encourage and Who Can Support and Encourage You

A woman was walking along the beach when she stumbled upon a genie's lamp. She picked it up and rubbed it and, lo and behold, a genie appeared. The amazed woman asked if she got three wishes.
The genie said, "Nope, due to inflation, constant downsizing, low wages in third world countries, and fierce global competition, I can only grant you one wish. So what'll it be?"

The woman didn't hesitate. She said, "I want peace in the Middle East. See this map? I want these countries to stop fighting with each other."

The genie looked at the map and exclaimed, "Gadzooks, lady! These countries have been at war for thousands of years. I'm good, but not that good! Please make another wish."

The woman thought for a minute and said, "Well, I've never been able to find the right man; one that's considerate and fun, likes to cook and helps with the housecleaning, is good in bed and gets along with my family, doesn't watch sports all the time, and is faithful."

The genie let out a long sigh and said, "Let me see that map again."

Marriage or a life partner relationship is one of the more important factors for many as to whether they will or will not become extraordinary. Actually, if you want to be extraordinary, you will probably be better off not getting married or forming a lasting relationship until your mid-thirties. As time goes by, people change a lot before hitting their mid-thirties. So, you may not end up with the person you expected or hoped that you would be getting.

However, once people reach their mid-thirties, they are unlikely to change very much. You need to be realistic and know if they are not on a solid career path by their mid-thirties, they probably will never be. If they have substance abuse issues, they will likely always be addicted to something. Of course, there are exceptions, but nothing is so ordinary as to believe you have come across the exception.

How many times have you heard the phrase, "opposites attract"? The reason you hear this phrase so often is that it is true. You want to select a life partner who is extraordinary, but in a way that is different from how you are extraordinary.

The trick is finding a life partner who is both your equal and yet different from you. By doing so, you exchange a competitive relationship that often comes with being outstanding in the same areas for a supportive relationship that comes from building on each other's strengths.

Equality is important in a lasting relationship. If your partner is dependent upon you, he or she will tend to drag you down or, at best, will refuse to believe you can rise to the heights of the extraordinary. If you are dependent upon your partner, you are automatically ordinary at best. You want someone you can respect and encourage as well as someone who respects and encourages you.

Be extraordinary by being careful to select a life partner who you can support and encourage and who can support and encourage you.

"In a relationship, each person should support the other; they should lift each other up."

Source: Taylor Swift

Marriage Film: *Marry Me*
Distributed by Fox (2012) (Japan) (TV) and
Lifetime Television (2010) (USA) (TV)

("Marry Me" is the story of Rae Carter (Lucy Liu), a former artist now working as a social worker, who has always believed in the fairy-tale romance... Description source: IMDB)

WEEK 51:

*Death—Consider Death Every Day so that You Can
Make the Most of Every Day*

<u>Two Ladies Talking in Heaven</u>

First woman: Hi Wanda!

Second woman: Hi Sylvia! How'd you die?

First woman: I froze to death.

Second woman: How horrible!

First woman: It wasn't so bad. After I quit shaking from the cold, I
began to get warm and sleepy, and then I finally died a peaceful death.
What about you?

Second woman: I died of a massive heart attack. I suspected that my husband was cheating, so I came home early to catch him in the act. Instead, I found him all by himself in the den watching TV.

First woman: So, what happened?

Second woman: I was so sure there was another woman there somewhere that I started running all over the house looking. I ran up into the attic and searched, and down into the basement. Then I went through every closet and checked under all the beds. I kept this up until I had looked everywhere, and finally I became so exhausted that I just keeled over with a heart attack and died.

First woman: Too bad, you didn't look in the freezer—we'd both still be alive.

Many ordinary people fear death and will give up much in exchange for a longer life, whereas the extraordinary person accepts death as part of the cycle of life.

That isn't to say that the extraordinary people will not make heroic struggles to stay alive, but they do it for the sake of others and not for themselves.

Extraordinary people treat everyone they meet with respect. They realize that today could be the last day of someone they interact with that day. Extraordinary people, being mindful of death each morning, try to make the most of every hour of every day.

Be extraordinary by being mindful that this could be your last day or the last day for someone you meet.

"Life is such a short journey.
Spend it being yourself."
Source: George Foreman

Death Film: *Meet Joe Black*
Distributed by Universal Pictures

(A media mogul acts as a guide to Death, who takes the form of a young man, to learn about life on Earth and in the process, fall in love with his guide's daughter. Description source: IMDB)

WEEK 52:

*Winning—Enjoy the Journey and Don't Be
Concerned with Your Destination*

A man is driving down a country road when he spots a farmer standing
in the middle of a huge field of grass. He pulls the car over to the side
of the road and notices that the farmer is just standing there, doing
nothing, looking at nothing.

The man gets out of the car, walks all the way out to the farmer, and
asks him, "Ah, excuse me mister, but what are you doing?"

The farmer replies, "I'm trying to win a Nobel Prize."

"How?" asks the man, puzzled.

"Well, I heard they give the Nobel Prize to people who are out standing
in their fields."

You will never ever be extraordinary until you stop being concerned with becoming a winner or even being extraordinary. The moment you stop caring is the moment you truly become extraordinary.

You should work hard at perfecting the above mentioned fifty-one traits so that you play the game of life to the best of your ability—that is all that matters, perfecting your abilities. Achieving perfection is not within a human's grasp. However, we can all strive for perfection. If you continuously strive toward perfection, without caring what others think, you will find yourself becoming extraordinary.

Be extraordinary. Simply enjoy the journey, and don't be concerned with the destination.

"What good is being the best, if it brings out the worst in you?"

Source: Rodney Dangerfield in 1992 film *Ladybugs*

Winning Film: *Invictus*
Distributed by Warner Bros. Pictures

(Nelson Mandela, in his first term as the South African President, initiates a unique venture to unite the apartheid-torn land: enlist the national rugby team on a mission to win the 1995 Rugby World Cup. Description source: IMDB)

FINAL THOUGHT

"Desiderata" by Max Ehrmann

Go placidly amid the noise and haste, and remember what peace
there may be in silence.

As far as possible, without surrender, be on good terms with all
persons.

Speak your truth quietly and clearly; and listen to others, even the
dull and the ignorant; they too have their story.

Avoid loud and aggressive persons; they are vexations to the spirit.

If you compare yourself with others,
you may become vain and bitter, for always there will be greater and
lesser persons than yourself.

Enjoy your achievements as well as your plans.

Keep interested in your own career, however humble; it is a real
possession in the changing fortunes of time.

Exercise caution in your business affairs,
for the world is full of trickery.
But let this not blind you to what virtue there is;
many persons strive for high ideals; and everywhere life is full of
heroism.

Be yourself.

Especially, do not feign affection.
Neither be cynical about love, for in the face of all aridity and
disenchantment it is as perennial as the grass.

Take kindly the counsel of the years, gracefully surrendering the
things of youth.

Nurture strength of spirit to shield you in sudden misfortune.
But do not distress yourself with dark imaginings.
Many fears are born of fatigue and loneliness.

Beyond a wholesome discipline, be gentle with yourself.

You are a child of the universe, no less than the trees and the stars;
you have a right to be here.
And whether or not it is clear to you, no doubt the universe is
unfolding, as it should.

Therefore be at peace with God, whatever you conceive Him to be.
And whatever your labors and aspirations, in the noisy confusion of
life, keep peace in your soul.

With all its sham, drudgery, and broken dreams,
it is still a beautiful world. Be cheerful.
Strive to be happy.

50034753R00121

Made in the USA
Lexington, KY
01 March 2016